WHEN
GEORGE
CAME TO EDINBURGH

WHEN
GEORGE
CAME TO EDINBURGH

JOHN NEIL MUNRO

BIRLINN

First published in 2010 by
Birlinn Limited
West Newington House
10 Newington Road
Edinburgh
EH9 1QS

www.birlinn.co.uk

ISBN: 978 1 84158 889 6

British Library Cataloguing-in-Publication Data
A catalogue record for this book is available from the British Library

Typeset by Iolaire Typesetting, Newtonmore
Printed and bound by MPG Books Ltd, Bodmin

This book is dedicated to the friends who gave it encouragement, especially DJ Murray and Spook.

* * *

Contents

INTRODUCTION

On the morning of Saturday, 10 November 1979, the people of Edinburgh woke to stories in their local newspaper of strange goings-on. Pride of place on the front page of the *Evening News* went to the peculiar tale of a 61-year-old forestry worker who had complained of being assaulted and threatened with abduction by 'strange creatures' in a dense wooded area near the town of Livingston. The man – who baffled detectives stressed was sober, of sound mind and impeccable integrity – told a tale that was as chilling as it was inexplicable.

While walking through the woods, he came across a 30-foot high spacecraft with a dome that constantly changed colours atop a platform with antennae. He was then attacked by two 'aliens' – with round bodies and at least six legs – which bore no resemblance to humans. They approached him silently and at great speed and made genuine efforts to drag him into the machine. The man told police that he became aware of a foul smell, promptly fainted and woke to find that the aliens had disappeared and that he had lost his voice and couldn't walk. He then had to crawl one-and-a-half miles to his home, from where he was subsequently taken to Bangour General Hospital.

At the site of the 'abduction', police found marks on the ground where leg struts of some machine weighing several tons had rested. The grass was pressed down in two parallel ladder-like patterns and there were four holes sunk deep into the soil indicating four supporting struts. It was generally agreed that no land-based machines that size could have penetrated so deeply into the forest and the marks did not bear resemblance to any land or airborne vehicle known to man.

It isn't known if the victim of the abduction attempt was a Hibernian fan, but you kind of hope he wasn't. Because if, after checking himself out of hospital, he had gone to Easter Road that Saturday, he would have seen another strange sight which would have added to his confusion. Striding along through the winter gloom that seemed to hang permanently over the old stadium in those days, past the Albion Road sauna and surrounded by a swarm of camera-wielding press hacks, was certainly the most glamorous and debatably the greatest-ever footballer to grace the game. And to make it even stranger, George Best, arm-in-arm with his gorgeous wife Angie, wasn't just making a social visit to the struggling Leith club. No, he was actually just about to discuss signing a contract that would see the most famous footballer of all time play for Hibs!

* * *

The coming together of George Best and Hibernian FC was one of the more bizarre episodes in the history of Scotland's national game. True, it's not quite as implausible as Dumbarton's brave but ultimately hopeless bid to sign the Dutch genius Johann Cruyff in 1980, but it comes close. Thirty years on, it still raises questions. Why did a man who could have played anywhere in the world choose to come to Scotland? And why did he decide to sign for Hibs, who were statistically only the tenth best team in the land in 1979, when the wise money would have been on him playing for Celtic or Rangers, the two clubs who had dominated the Scottish game for most of the twentieth century? And once he signed, what went wrong? How did he end up getting suspended and then sacked by Hibs? How did George blow the final chance to resurrect his career and to achieve one of his great ambitions – to perform on the biggest stage of all and play at a World Cup? Hopefully, this book will answer these questions and also correct a few of the myths that surround George's time in Edinburgh.

Hibs have been habitual underachievers, but that particular year they were experiencing a season from hell. Rooted at the foot of the table after one-third of the season, they needed a miracle worker. Instead, they signed a depressed, lonely, faded superstar who was fighting a losing battle with alcoholism.

In the many books written about Best, there's been very little mention of his Edinburgh episode, and the cynics will probably say that the biographers have got it right. They'll argue that he only played a handful of games, only scored a few goals and failed to save Hibs from relegation. But the cynics are wrong. In the end, George was a Hibs player for just 36 days short of a year and he even came back the next season to play for Hibs in the old First Division. And although he may have been a shadow of his former self, he still managed to conjure up moments of breathtaking brilliance. If he had spent the year at either of the Old Firm teams, you would never have heard the end of it and his stay would have been the subject of countless books, stage plays and possibly even a light opera. But because he played with Hibs, his year tends to be belittled and passed over.

Looking back on George's time in Edinburgh, sometimes you don't know whether to laugh or cry at what he got up to. On the one hand, his drinking and womanising have elevated George to patron saint of the lad culture, but it should never be forgotten that his alcoholism caused a great deal of grief to those who loved him most. So in retelling the story of his year in Scotland, this book will try to avoid glorifying or being judgemental about his exploits. Instead, it is a straight narrative of what actually happened through the recollections of George, Angie and more than 20 people who played with him, drank with him or just stood on the terraces to watch him play.

Another rich source of information was the newspapers of the time. Whatever his personal problems, George could still play the press like no one else. There was a time in early 1980 when it seemed that every day the national newspapers carried a photo – usually on the front page – of a pensive-looking George at Edinburgh or London airport having just been sacked or suspended. All the big-selling dailies and Sundays boasted regular 'exclusive' photos and stories with the star. The *Daily Express*, back in the day when it led the middle market newspapers, had a weekly Monday column where George offered his personal views on his own frailties.

* * *

Special thanks go to Angie Best for taking time to answer all my questions and to all those who gave their memories of meeting George or of seeing him play. Thanks also to those who couldn't help, but knew a man who could. I'm thinking of the likes of Stephen Rafferty, Rab McNeil of *The Herald*, Sandie McIver (Edinburgh) and Norrie Muir, and to Ally Clark and Callum Ian MacMillan for their help. Gratitude goes, too, to Neville Moir, Peter Burns and all the rest of the Birlinn team, Richie Wilson my editor, Kate Pool from the Society of Authors, and staff at Stornoway Library, the National Library of Scotland and the British Library Newspaper Reading Room (Colindale, London).

GGTTH
John Neil, February 2010

CHAPTER ONE

GENIUS

George Best always wanted to be remembered for his football abilities rather than his off-the-field activities. So before describing the occasional madness and sadness of his year in Edinburgh, it's only right to recall that at his peak in the mid-1960s, George was an awesome football player. The boy from Burren Way on the Cregagh Estate in Belfast had it all. Equally strong on either foot, he was beautifully balanced and lightning fast, with an ability to deliver pinpoint passes from all angles and distances. He had tantalising ball control, possessed a body swerve that could destroy opposing defences and could shoot crisply and accurately from any distance. Best was also a strong and fearless tackler; indeed Old Trafford boss Sir Matt Busby always said that George was the best tackler in his great Manchester United team of the 1960s – and this in a side that featured pitbulls like Nobby Stiles and Pat Crerand. To round things off, George was also good in the air and pretty handy in front of goal, scoring 178 times in 464 appearances for United. The sight of George lacerating a defence is one that will always stick in the memory. Best's favourite football writer, Geoffrey Green of *The Times*, got it right when he once memorably described George, aged just 19, 'gliding like a dark ghost' past Benfica defenders in a 1966 European Cup tie.

George's football talent was spotted at an early age by Bob Bishop, Manchester United's chief scout in Northern Ireland, who famously sent a telegram to Busby which read: 'I think I've found you a genius.' George overcame doubts about his slight frame and his own homesickness to sign as a professional for

United on £17 a week in 1963. The teenage starlet was obsessed with football and dedicated to his craft; he loved to train and to help those around him. George claimed that – as a callow teenager – he could beat his teammates in training sprints running backwards, while they ran forwards! Rigorous workouts helped build up his weight to 10 stone 3lbs, which was to remain fairly constant throughout his glory days at Old Trafford. George was also, as even the most heterosexual male would have to admit, a very handsome man. With his athletic build, boyish good looks, shock of black hair and designer stubble, George had that unique quality – men wanted to be his best friend and women wanted to marry him. The chat-show host Michael Parkinson, who knew many a handsome movie star and sportsman, says that George was the biggest babe-magnet of them all. The Irishman used to wear a gold chain around his neck with the simple wording 'Yes', which presumably helped him to cut out unnecessary conversation on his nights out pulling women.

George and Michael Parkinson. *The Scotsman*

His amazing displays during the early years of his career peaked in 1968, when he played a starring role in United's 4–1 win over Benfica in the European Cup final. But his behaviour after the game on the night that should have been his greatest triumph revealed the extent of his growing drink problem. Many years later, he confessed that he could not remember anything of the post-match celebrations in London's West End. His drinking, which he attributed to his own shyness and inability to come to terms with his pop star status, grew progressively worse, and by his own account he was an alcoholic by 1972. (Unfortunately, this admission only came later in life; when he arrived in Edinburgh George was still in denial and refusing to admit that he had a drink problem.) George's speciality was three or four-day binges to 'forget about everything' – these drinking bouts usually arrived without warning and invariably at times when things were looking positive for George. He once told the ITV football programme *On the Ball*: 'I want to be the best at everything, even boozing. That's my nature.' If the party lasted for four hours then George would stay for five. And when he was drinking, nothing else mattered, not even money. He once lost out on a TV commercial that would have paid him £20,000, just because he was due to have a drinking session with his mates on the same day as the advert was to be shot.

The binge drinking continued off and on throughout the rest of his life. Through the 1970s, George's alcoholism became an ugly spectator sport that just about everyone in Britain had a view on. His career had turned into something of a freak show after he walked out on Manchester United for the last time in December 1973. A couple of years later, he was hawking his wares at Dunstable Town in the Southern League. Then he moved on to Stockport County, Los Angeles Aztecs and Cork Celtic before finally finding a semblance of happiness at Fulham in 1976, playing alongside another pair of faded superstars in Bobby Moore and Rodney Marsh. But, predictably, when things got difficult at Craven Cottage, George did a runner back to Los Angeles. While Fulham languished in sixteenth place in Division Two, George was content to go on three to four-day long binges in shabby Los

George with Manchester United manager Tommy Docherty. *Getty Images*

Angeles bars. By 1979, George was at his lowest ebb and playing fitfully for the Fort Lauderdale Strikers in the NASL. His long-suffering wife, Angie, had walked out on him (only to return shortly afterwards) with the famous line: 'You're wasting your life George, you're not going to waste mine as well.' Best was starting to resemble a tramp, occasionally sleeping on beaches between drinking bouts. He was also wracked with guilt over the death of his mother Ann in October 1978. Like her famous son, Mrs Best had a serious drink problem that contributed to her dying from heart disease. George blamed himself for not being there when his mother needed him most and he became increasingly depressed, finding it difficult to share his true feelings with others.

In previous years, he could always escape from his worries on the football pitch. Now, even that option was starting to fade away. Manchester United had cruelly said no to a testimonial for the club's most famous son and Best understandably felt annoyed by the refusal. Around this time, he also unwittingly broke the terms of his registration by playing some invitation matches for an American team in Europe and was banned by the football authority FIFA from playing anywhere in the world. Although the ban was eventually lifted, it helped contribute to the image of George as yesterday's man. Running out of options stateside, George returned to England eager to settle down, and initially moved to Southend to live with Angie and her parents. Still registered with Fulham, who allowed him to train with the first-team squad at the Bank of England sports ground in Roehampton, Best had appeared on ITV's *World of Sport* to say he would play for free with any English First Division team to prove his worth. There were no takers. George talked about interest from eight English clubs, including two First Division teams, but in reality there was no sign of a contract being offered. So when Hibs chairman Tom Hart came calling, Best must have thought, 'what have I got to lose?' Angie Best recalls: 'When Hibs got in contact, it was a desperation point for George. He was at a very low ebb. George was always keen on any idea or offer that would help him to get better, because he never knew how to help himself, he kept failing and failing, and the offer from Hibs came at an ideal moment.' Vowing, not for the first – or last – time, to give up the booze, Best accepted the Hibs offer. So the man described as the most exciting footballer and most frustrating employee of his day ended up at Easter Road. In one sense, it wasn't wholly a leap into the unknown: the Best family had Scottish roots. George's paternal grandfather, James 'Scottie' Best, was raised in Glasgow and worked for some time at the Clyde shipyards before returning to Belfast to work at Harland and Wolff. During his son's year in Edinburgh, George's father made frequent visits to Scotland and apparently felt right at home and had many friends here, especially in Glasgow.*

When he signed for Hibs, Best was already well into the downward spiral which would eventually leave him bankrupt and beaten by alcoholism. Vodka was his poison of choice, and he could pack it away with frightening ease: he once drank a pint of the stuff in one go just to win a bet. Jim Blair, the late, great *Daily Record* columnist, once said that George was the type of guy that even the Samaritans would hang up the phone on. A trifle harsh, but George did have an uncanny knack of messing up just when it seemed easier to do the right thing. Angie had done her best to sort out his financial affairs and help his fight against alcoholism, but it wasn't easy: they had already split up four times since their marriage in 1978, only to get together again and soldier on. It also couldn't help that George's life away from football revolved around licensed premises. Even near the end of his spell in Edinburgh, he still had a one-third share in a bar on Hermosa Beach in LA and substantial interests in two nightclubs – Slack Alice's and Oscar's in Manchester.

But as is often the way, the public seemed to love him all the more because of his flaws; there was something reassuring that someone with so much talent could also have the same weaknesses as the ordinary bloke on the street. Although his problems often got the better of him, George was at heart a good person. As his sister Barbara described him: self-effacing, down to earth,

---

* Angie Best's mother is also Scottish.

mild-mannered and not at all pretentious. All these attributes were to the fore during his time in Edinburgh. As teammate Jackie McNamara says: 'He was a marvellous guy and everyone really liked him.' The public could also see that, unlike many of his fellow footballers, George was an intelligent man. Anyone who heard him speak on the chat show *Parkinson* in the 1970s will recall him as witty and eloquent. He was a keen reader with an offbeat taste in fiction – one person I spoke to remembers George being aware of the Jerzy Kosinski novel *Being There* long before it was adapted into a film starring Peter Sellers. George also had a keen interest in biographies; in one interview, he said: 'I am fascinated by Hitler and the mass murderer Charles Manson – they were evil but radiated fantastic power.' George himself harboured little-known but genuine writing ambitions – he told one reporter that his dream was to own a 20-bedroom hotel where he could write novels.

A one-year contract with Hibs allowed George to train in London during the week and then fly up to Edinburgh on Thursday, train with the rest of the squad on Friday and fly back to London on the Saturday night. But as Ally MacLeod, Hibs' top striker back then, told me, this arrangement was hardly conducive to getting the best out of the mercurial Northern Irishman. Ally and several of the other older heads at Easter Road had reservations about the signing, although they were soon won over by the star's homespun personality and his ability on the pitch.

Following a pattern set throughout his career, George initially knuckled down, training hard and staying sober. When he was in the right mindset, he actually loved working on the pitch and the feeling of getting fit again. And when he did turn up for the Hibs training sessions, he worked overtime with younger players on improving their skills. Hibs' manager Eddie Turnbull gave Best the No. 11 shirt and a free role on the pitch, but with his main position being left of midfield behind the strikers. His arrival immediately lifted a squad beset by self-doubt. But he was more than a stone overweight and both his ankles were bloated after years of being hacked by journeymen full-backs. One fan, the MSP Iain Gray, told me how near the end of games, George seemed to gravitate towards the tunnel so he didn't have too far to walk at full-time.

Best's year at Hibs saw his physical condition deteriorate further. While in London or Manchester, he was drinking and not bothering to train so the couple of days – at most – he spent training in Edinburgh were never going to be sufficient to get him fit for the hard grind of a winter playing in the Scottish Premier League. And the more he drank, the more depressed and lonely he became. Sadly, his time at Hibs is often remembered more for him going AWOL – or as he called it 'going on the missing list' – generating frustration rather than excitement. On one occasion, he set off for the airport, then decided he couldn't be bothered and stayed in London boozing. Another time, he actually managed to arrive at Edinburgh airport, only to catch the next flight back down south.

If he was a Rolls Royce in his heyday, George was more like a Vauxhall Cavalier by the time he arrived at Easter Road. Those ex-Hibs players who were interviewed for this book almost always mentioned how, although he still had the ability to do things other footballers could only dream of, he had 'lost the pace'. Also, his shoulder blade was just recovering from being fractured during his time at Fulham, when he crashed a borrowed Alfa Romeo car at 4 a.m. after a night boozing. He wrapped the expensive vehicle around a lamppost outside Harrods and also had to have 57 stitches in his face as a result of the smash. Eddie Turnbull rated George at his peak as one of the all-time greats, along with Cruyff, Maradona and Pele, but Turnbull was secretly dead against the Irishman's move to Easter Road. In his biography, Turnbull recalls the moment when he looked George straight in the face and saw damaged goods: 'His blue eyes had the look of a hard drinker about them, the yellowing skin around them a sure sign. I had seen plenty of faces like it in my career, and there was no mistaking the signs of someone who was on the skids.'

If George Best had any genuine hopes of kicking the booze into touch, then Edinburgh was not the ideal place for him to move to in 1979. Then, as now, Scotland's capital was one of the champion drinking cities in Europe. George had a wide range of licensed

premises to choose from. Annabel's on Semple Street was the city's
most luxurious nightclub/disco – the only establishment in the UK
to boast 24-carat gold-plated tables and chairs, it was open every

George, the centre of attention. *Scran*

night of the week until 3 a.m. At the other end of the luxury scale,
the Clan Bar, Dizzy Lizzie's, and the Royal Nip were some of Leith's
more notorious hostelries. The Clan on Albert Street occasionally
pulled in the punters with male go-go dancers. The sight of those
dancers never really leaves the memory – if you didn't need a drink
before seeing them, you certainly needed one afterwards.

To begin with, George stayed at the North British Hotel (also known as the NB and now the Balmoral) at the east end of Princes Street, an imposing and luxurious Edwardian building which attracted the very rich and famous. If Tom Hart was trying to keep Best on the straight and narrow, he couldn't have picked a worse place. The NB's own bars were impressive enough, but the hotel was also within walking distance of many of Edinburgh's finest watering holes, including the Café Royal and the pubs of Rose Street. The *Daily Express* journalist Andy McInnes told Stephen McGowan how when he once interviewed the star in the NB hotel, the waiter brought George his 'usual' – what appeared to be a large glass of Coke. 'Only when I went to pay the bill and studied the receipt,' McInnes recalls, 'did I notice that he had four vodkas poured into the Coke. No wonder it looked so large. And this was his usual.'

The Hibs players' own pubs of choice were Sinclair's on Montrose Terrace (now the Terrace Inn), Leerie's Lamplighter on Dublin Street on Saturday nights and Jinglin' Geordie's* during the week. The latter pub, on the city's Fleshmarket Close, was also a favourite hang-out of hacks from *The Scotsman* and *Evening News* who only had to sway a few steps from their back door to the pub. The Jinglin's landlord back then, David Scrimgeour, gave me a quick history of the tiny wee bar that was to become synonymous with George Best.

'Jinglin' Geordie's used to be a pub called the Suburban Bar and it was a right honky-tonk slum of a place,' he said. 'A great pal of mine at the time was the chairman of Bass the brewers and when I was chatting to him one day about journalism and our favourite hostelries, he asked me if I ever thought of running a pub myself. I initially said no, but eventually I ended up getting the Suburban Bar and the brewers very kindly demolished the interior and did it up to a very high standard. The place used to be mobbed all the time – I

---

* The Jinglin' Geordie pub is named after George Heriot, jeweller and goldsmith to King James VI. Heriot amassed a considerable fortune during his lifetime and earned his nickname as he ran beside the king's coach with coins jingling in his pockets. A bequest in his will founded George Heriot's private school in the capital.

had four staff on the go continuously. There were 1,500 employees at *The Scotsman* building who were all well paid, and a fair proportion of them liked a drink, plus we catered for all the traders from the Fruitmarket.'

The mix of journalists and footballers meant that Edinburgh was soon ablaze with rumours of what the Irish playboy was getting up to in his spare time. The intentions of some of the reporters weren't always honourable. Friends remember a 'conveyor belt' of women waiting their turn to meet George. Different people I spoke to remember the effect he had on the female population of Edinburgh, with old grannies going weak at the knees in his presence. Others just gravitated towards him, stretched out a hand to touch him and then retreated back to their seats without saying a word.

CHAPTER TWO

JOURNEYMEN

Being a Hibs fan has never been a job for the glory hunter. Founded in 1875 by the Irish community in Scotland's capital, the club had lasted for 104 years before George Best arrived on the scene and in all those years, Hibs had won just seven major competitions: four League Championships, two Scottish Cups and one Scottish League Cup. It's the type of record that leads fans to adopt a stoical attitude. A good sense of humour helps, too. Edinburgh-born war veteran John 'Jock' Wilson spent almost a century watching Hibs before his death in 2008, aged 105, and he knew better than most that following the Leith outfit requires a strong sense of self-deprecatory humour. Commenting on the Military Medal earned on active service, Jock would quip: 'Well, I didn't get it for following Hibs for 90 years – that would deserve the Victoria Cross.' The comedian Bill Barclay, who was born and raised in Leith and has been a Hibee all his life, once joked: 'I remember the last time we were in Europe, the fans let us down coming back on the ferry. They pulled down all the sails and threw the canons over the side.'

But the gallows humour and bare statistics don't tell the whole story. For all their occasional spells of mediocrity, Hibs have frequently had a reputation for innovation and for playing free-flowing expressive football. In the decade following the end of the Second World War, they won three league titles. Back then, their forward line – nicknamed The Famous Five – were a wonder to behold. Bobby Johnstone, Willie Ormond, Lawrie Reilly, Eddie Turnbull and Gordon Smith were feared and respected throughout Europe. Fast-forward 20 years and Eddie Turnbull as manager at Easter Road put together another mighty side. Known as Turnbull's

Tornadoes, Hibs in the 1970s were a team laced with entertainers, and names like John Brownlie, Pat Stanton, Alex Cropley, Alex Edwards, Alan Gordon and Jimmy O'Rourke are still revered down Leith way. Stanton in particular was a class act. Simon Pia, who has written a couple of great books about Hibs, told me: 'For most fans of my generation, there can only be one man – Patrick Gordon Stanton. A great tackler and passer of the ball, Pat was also a goalscorer and particularly good in the air. He played with elegance, with his head up and always seemed to have so much time, reading the game so well.'

Stanton's Hibs triumphed twice in the now defunct Drybrough Cup and also won the League Cup once with a stirring 2–1 win over Celtic in season 1972–73. That victory was the Tornadoes' finest performance, with Pat Stanton providing a peerless display, outshining a Celtic side that contained legendary names like Danny McGrain, Kenny Dalglish and Jimmy Johnstone. The Tornadoes also reached the Scottish Cup final in 1972 and had some memorable nights in Europe throughout the 1970s. A good deal of the credit for the team's success must go to their manager, Eddie Turnbull. As Jackie McNamara, who came to Easter Road in an unpopular swap deal which saw Pat Stanton go to Celtic, recalls: 'As a manager, Eddie Turnbull was second to none. He's the best I ever worked under. I don't like to draw comparisons with [Jock] Stein because I worked with Big Jock near the end of his career and in a way he had already done it all, maybe the hunger wasn't really there for him anymore. Turnbull would put you into a situation in training and 99 times out of 100 when you played on a Saturday that training situation would help you deal with the real thing during the match. He could be a hard man, but I was a bit of a favourite of his because of all the stick he got when he signed me. But Pat Stanton ended up retiring the season that he signed for Celtic and Turnbull got another ten years out of me.'

By the end of the 1970s, the great Hibs team had mostly gone their separate ways, lured from Edinburgh by the prospect of higher wages and more regular success on the field. John Brownlie and John Blackley had headed to Newcastle, Blackley for £100,000 and

Brownlie leaving as part of the deal which took Ralph Callachan to Easter Road. O'Rourke, Gordon and Edwards had also moved on and even promising youngsters like Bobby Smith – who was sold to Leicester City – were also being shipped out of Leith. What was left was a shadow of the early 1970s outfit. Part-time chiropodist Arthur Duncan was one of the few remaining from the great side, but even he had reverted from being a buccaneering winger to a full-back with licence to overlap.

Arthur Duncan. *Copyright unknown*

Ian Wood, who has worked at *The Scotsman* for 40 years, was a regular in the Easter Road press box back in the 1970s and remembers that one signing in particular seemed to set Hibs back.

'Eddie Turnbull had built a tremendous side but for some reason or other, I never found out why, they started to change that team. It all started to go wrong when they signed Joe Harper from Everton.

I'm not blaming Joe, he had some good performances for Hibs, but after he signed the morale of the team went through the floor. I think they dropped Alan Gordon to make way for Joe, even though Alan was an integral part of that team, scoring lots of goals – he had been in the running for the European Golden Boot award. That side was never quite the same again and by 1979 they were a shadow of their former selves; in terms of the great Hibs teams of the past, they were sub-standard.'

Stanton's departure for Celtic was the bitterest pill for Hibs fans to swallow and Jackie McNamara learnt pretty quickly just how fickle the Hibs fans could be. But having being born in Possilpark and raised in Easterhouse, two of Glasgow's most notorious schemes, Jackie took it all in his stride.

'Coming to Hibs initially was very difficult for me, especially as I didn't know I was getting swapped for another human being, like going back to the slave trade days. It was all hush-hush; I had been in to see Jock Stein in the Celtic Park boardroom and had signed for Hibs. When I walked out, I saw Pat Stanton waiting to go in with his old teammate, Alan Gordon, who was his agent. I just thought, "what's going on here?"

'At the time I was more or less on the scrap heap, I had my cruciate ligament hanging by a thread and Big Jock was glad to get rid of me and get Pat in. Fortunately for me, Hibs didn't pump me with cortisone like Celtic had done. The first few games I played for Hibs, the fans were booing me every time I went near the ball. In fact, the booing actually started before I arrived. The day I signed, Celtic were playing Dundee United and I was advised by Big Jock to go through and see my new team, but I said, "no, I've been here five years so I want to say goodbye to my mates here". That same night, Hibs were playing Montrose and the fans were booing all the time because they heard Stanton was going.

'I got injured after about ten games with Hibs and they got me an operation which kept me out of circulation for a good six months. When I came back, it was like Hibs were getting a new player and all the booing stopped, people started saying "ah, he's no as bad as we thought he was". These first games weren't easy though – you have to be thick-skinned to get through it, but I had been through all the political stuff at Celtic, condemning the bigotry and all that nonsense.'

Long after leaving Easter Road, George Best was less than complimentary about the standard of the Hibs team he played with, dismissing them as 'a poor side, with no decent players'. In truth, they may not have had the class of Bobby Charlton or Denis Law, but Best's judgement was very harsh. In the season prior to his arrival, Hibs had only narrowly missed out on qualifying for Europe and also managed to reach the Scottish Cup final.

On the way to Hampden, Hibs had beaten Hearts 2–1 at Tynecastle in the quarter-final and then edged out Aberdeen by the same score in the semi-final. Subsequently, though, they went off the boil and even took a 6–1 hammering from Partick Thistle in a league game. So in the final they were underdogs against a Rangers team on the rise: packed with experience and with two outstanding youngsters in Bobby Russell and Davie Cooper. It ended up 0–0: a dull game in which, as *The Scotsman* commented, 'not much happened with continued regularity'. Hibs might have snatched a win in the dying minutes, though, when Hebridean striker Colin Campbell gathered a through ball from Ally MacLeod and thumped a swerving drive which Peter McLoy in the Rangers goal did superbly well to deflect wide. Campbell was also denied a penalty with just minutes to go when he knocked the ball past McLoy only to be brought down. But in fairness, Rangers had their own chances and Derek Parlane could have won it for the Glasgow men in 69 minutes when he hit the underside of the crossbar.

More than 50,000 watched the first game, but the replay only drew less than 33,000. Those who stayed away made the wise choice and by the end of the second 0–0 game even the most die-hard Hibs and Rangers fans were losing the will to live. One press box observer said that the final – played out in dismal weather conditions – was beginning to rival *Gone with the Wind* as the longest-running entertainment in living memory. Still, Hibs had their chances and finished the stronger side, with Higgins, Bremner, MacLeod and Rae all missing good opportunities. Eventually, a second replay 12 days later at Hampden saw the deadlock broken. This time, Hibs grabbed two goals through Tony Higgins (the first goal of the final scored after 226 minutes of play) and Ally MacLeod, but in the end an Arthur Duncan own-goal as he tried and failed to deal with a Davie Cooper cross consigned them to a cruel 3–2 defeat. Ian Wood told readers of *The Scotsman* that the final came to life in a period of extra-time that 'had everything apart from an earthquake'. For the small band of Hibees gathered on the rain-lashed East terracing, the manner of defeat was cruel in the extreme. They were well aware that they hadn't won the Scottish Cup since the days of the Boer War (1902, to be precise), but consoled themselves with the thought that another win was inevitable soon. Thirty years on and they are still waiting.

Hibs striker Tony Higgins told me that defeat weighed heavy on the minds of the players. 'By the end of the 1970s, certainly in terms of the status of the team, the quality wasn't as good as it had been a few years earlier. We had been in the cup final the previous season and we probably should have won that game. The new season promised so much but we got off to a really bad start. Maybe losing that cup final was a bigger blow than we realised at the time.' Jackie McNamara adds: 'They were poor games but we probably should have won them. The powers that be thought things were OK in the squad because we got to the cup final, whereas in reality we got there because of Eddie Turnbull's tactical ability. The two really good players in the squad were Ally MacLeod and Des Bremner, who was sold to Aston Villa and went on to win the League and European Cup with them. When he left, that was our engine room away. We got two lads in from Leeds and the boys just never cut it at Hibs. We also got Joe Ward in the swap deal for Des Bremner. Big Joe is a lovely lad but what we needed was another Des Bremner, so there was a lack of investment in the squad.'

Still, the team that started the 1979 season had its fair share of strength, experience and youthful self-confidence. One or two of the players had the ability to perform at a much higher level. Eddie Turnbull – not a man to dish out praise unnecessarily – once went as far to describe regular goal-scorer Alisdair 'Ally' MacLeod as a genius. Jackie McNamara was also maturing into a fine player, having finally won over the Stanton-diehards on the terracing. But despite the talent at his disposal, Turnbull was shrewd enough to know that the squad needed an urgent injection of quality in order to prosper, and wanted the club to invest in a few decent players rather than go for the quick fix of a big-name signing. His calls went unheeded.

Though Turnbull managed the side, the man who really called the shots at Easter Road, and who made the decision to gamble on a move for George Best, was club chairman and majority shareholder Tom Hart. A millionaire who had made his fortune through his eponymous building firm, Hart had won control of the club back in September 1970 when he was just 48. The son of a Tranent miner, Hart was a talented schools footballer who had boyhood ambitions to play for the Hibees, but instead learned his trade as a bricklayer. He saw active service during the Second World War with the 8th Battalion, the Royal Scots, before being discharged after receiving a leg wound at Escaut Canal in September 1944 – an injury that effectively put paid to thoughts of a career in football. After ten years of hard graft during the day and evening studies at Heriot-Watt College, Hart founded his own business in 1954, eventually going public in 1968. The epitome of a self-made millionaire and a genuine hard worker, he turned a £100 war service gratuity into a fortune estimated at over £2.2 million in 20 years in the building trade. After selling his business to Crudens, he enjoyed the trappings of success, owning a home in Paguera, Majorca and making regular visits to the French Riviera. Where Hibs were concerned, Hart freely admitted to being a 'benevolent dictator', surrounding himself with his own men in the boardroom. Hart's own family owned 1,400 out of a total of 2,000 shares in the club and the chairman himself guaranteed the club to the tune of £70,000 at the bank. Jackie McNamara recalls: 'Tom Hart was Mr Hibs; he just wanted the best for the players and for the club. If he found out that Hearts were on £150 to beat us, he would put us on £250, that's the way he was.'

By the end of the 1970s, Hart had ploughed upwards of

£250,000 into the club, with very little prospect of getting it back. And having made that investment, Hart was never shy of letting his feelings be known. A lively and outspoken legislator, he was a member of the League Management Committee, the SFA council, and the Referee Committee – making him one of the most powerful men, outwith the Old Firm, in Scottish Football. During the 1979–80 season, he 'declared war' on the small number of Hibs fans who sang pro-IRA songs at games. As the name suggests, Hibernian had strong Irish roots, but Hart was having none of it and instructed police to eject anyone heard singing the songs or even waving the Irish tricolour at games.* During Hart's reign, Hibs earned a reputation for being innovators. In 1977, they became the first British side to have on-shirt sponsorship through a deal with the sportswear firm Bukta, and three years later they became the first Scottish club to install under-soil heating. When he signed George Best, Hart told the Irishman, 'let me down once and I'll clobber you'. In the end, George let him down more than once, but Hart came out of the whole affair with dignity in the way that he tried to help George.

Best arrived at a stadium that – like the club – had seen better days. In its heyday after the Second World War, the ground hosted massive crowds; in fact the record attendance of 65,840 was for a game against city rivals Hearts in January 1950. Even by 1979, the official capacity was more than 50,000, though there was never any danger of that figure being reached. The old ground had stands that were right by the touchline and the players were within earshot of every insult hurled their way. The main stand had a large top tier of seating with a standing enclosure beneath. The only other covered and seated area was in the Albion Road end of the ground, but even there wasn't a very comfortable place to sit when a mid-winter wind

* An interesting side issue is that George Best's father was a master of his local Orange lodge, though George was never one to place too much store in anyone's religion – someone's creed or colour was never an issue with him. George's family were from Protestant Free Presbyterian working-class stock and he grew up in a Belfast just on the brink of the sectarian troubles of 1960s and '70s. But throughout his life, George remained refreshingly free of the bigotry that stained his native land.

was whipping around the stadium. The massive uncovered east terracing was a throwback to the days when Hibs were a force in European football, but by 1979 it was sparsely populated and only good for offering fine views up to Arthur's Seat and over the Forth. The Dunbar Road end was similarly large, uncovered and empty, apart from the days that Celtic, Rangers and Hearts visited. But however much the stadium had fallen into disrepair, it remained a special place for the fans and all I spoke to can vividly recall the old ground, with its infamous slope and towering east terrace.

Mr Hibs, Tom Hart with George. *Mirrorpix*

CHAPTER THREE

THE SEASON FROM HELL

Just a few weeks before the start of the new season, Tom Hart told the press of his plans for major ground improvements at Easter Road and revealed that the club raked in over £100,000 from the marathon cup final against Rangers. Hibs fans expecting to see the money spent on major new signings were in for a big disappointment though. In the weeks leading up to the first day of the new season, the only new arrivals were David Reid and David Whyte – two young Scots who had failed to settle at Leeds United – and Jim Brown, the veteran former Hearts defender who was picked up on a free transfer. The signing of a young chemistry student from Edinburgh University – the speedy forward Derick Rodier – completed the summer transfer activity, but Hibs fans refused to hang out the bunting in celebration.

After pre-season training came the campaign's one and only meeting with deadly city rivals Hearts. It was part of the Skol Festival Trophy, a long-forgotten pre-season tournament which pitted the Edinburgh clubs against Coventry City and Manchester City. Hibs came into the derby game having already crashed out of the Anglo-Scottish Cup 4–3 on aggregate to St Mirren, but the 11,000 fans that turned up at Easter Road saw the home side win 2–1 with goals by Rae and Campbell. The *Evening News* hailed the 'discovery of the day' as 19-year-old Hibs centre-half Craig Paterson, son of 1950s Hibs defender John Paterson. Hearts battled dourly, but the goals and glory went to the Hibees – little did the fans know that they had just watched the high point of the season.

The rest of the Skol Trophy was a non-event, though there was real drama in the second game when Hibs' young striker, Colin

Campbell, collided with Manchester City's massive keeper, Joe Corrigan. Campbell swallowed his tongue and his life was saved by the trainers of both teams (the Hibs trainer was John Lambie, who went on to great fame as Partick Thistle manager and a pigeon fancier). Campbell was rushed to the local Royal Infirmary, where he was detained overnight, suffering from concussion and a bruised shoulder. Hibs meantime grabbed a 1–1 draw with City, Jim Brown winning over some of the Hibs fans with a glorious goal. Two days later, a commendable 0–0 draw with Coventry City earned Hibs the runners-up spot.

The new season arrived on Saturday, 11 August and Hibs started as they meant to go on, getting beaten 3–1 by Rangers. This was no disgrace, as the Gers had Davie Cooper, one of the few Scots players in recent history to be accurately described as a genius, on their side. Cooper scored a magnificent solo effort after Alex MacDonald had opened the scoring. Bobby Russell added a third while Gordon Rae countered for Hibs. Off the field, bottles flew among the fans and a young supporter was led away with blood streaming from his face. One week later, Hibs hit the bottom of the table following a 3–0 loss against Aberdeen at Pittodrie. Callachan and Campbell both hit the woodwork for the Edinburgh men, but defensive blunders cost them dear. In the final game of August, Hibs hauled themselves above Dundee and St Mirren with a 5–2 thumping of Dundee. One of the favourite songs of the Hibs faithful includes the line, 'We are Hibernian FC. We hate Jam Tarts and we hate Dundee.' In truth, Hibs fans don't really hate Dundee any more than any other provincial Scottish club, but the song got a full airing as Hibs reverted to the glory days of the early 1970s in a performance crowned by a superb solo effort by Ralph Callachan, who beat defender after defender before slipping the ball coolly into the net. Sadly, only 7,334 supporters were there to witness the Edinburgh side's first five-goal haul for 17 months. The following Wednesday, only 3,600 turned up to see Hibs booed off the pitch after a laboured 2–1 win over Montrose in the League Cup.

A trip to Rugby Park on 8 September ended in a 1–0 defeat against Kilmarnock. Hibs should have won, but a goal by Iain

Jardine two minutes from time spelt disaster. The following week, Hibs offered £150,000 for Airdrie's Sandy Clark. The striker showed some foresight in turning down the bid, preferring to stay part-time at Airdrie and earn good money as the manager of a credit company. Later, he did make the move to Edinburgh, but only to join Hearts, where he regularly helped his fellow striker John Robertson to put Hibs to the sword throughout the 1980s.

On 15 September, Tony Higgins gave Hibs the lead at home to Celtic. When Ally MacLeod stepped up to take a penalty, the Hibs faithful in the 20,001 crowd could only envisage one outcome, as Ally hadn't failed to convert a penalty in 13 attempts. He missed. Then Hibs folded spectacularly, allowing Lennox, Conroy and Murdo MacLeod with a penalty to put Celtic on easy street. The normally reliable Jackie McNamara messed up for the second goal and Ally Brazil did the same for Celtic's third, handling the ball while keeper Jim McArthur stood right behind him. Soon afterwards, droves of Hibs fans headed to the local bars for consolation.

To add to their woes, Hibs then sold their most influential playmaker. Des Bremner became the latest promising youngster to exit Easter Road – joining a long list which included names like Colin Stein, Peter Marinello and Alex Cropley. Hibs let it be known that the Highlander had actually submitted a transfer request the previous season and had made regular visits to Turnbull's office to reinforce his desire to leave. So when Aston Villa offered £275,000, it was time for Des to depart for the Midlands. Bremner's industry and talents were never truly replaced and Hibs' season soon went into freefall.

Turnbull used an estimated £80,000 of the Bremner fee to take striker Joe Ward back to Scotland from an unhappy spell at Villa. A former Scotland schoolboy cap, Ward had made his name as a regular goalscorer with Clyde. He jumped at the prospect of moving to Hibs, but sadly things did not work out and – to this day – the mere mention of the name Joe Ward can send some Hibs fans stretching for the sedatives. Hibs never won a game in which he played and he failed to score in any of his 11 appearances. Every striker has an off season, and this was Joe's.

More misery and defensive chaos followed as Hibs lost 2–0 at home to St Mirren on 22 September. Jimmy Bone and Frank McDougall scored for the Buddies, but really it could have been much more, with Hibs players making elementary blunders and being overrun in defence. For the first time, the R-word was mentioned around the ground. Turnbull was booed off the pitch by fans suddenly fearful of relegation.

The dreadful run of results continued when Kilmarnock rolled into town having never won at Easter Road in 15 years. This time, they won 2–1 in the first leg of a League Cup tie in front of only 4,321 fans. Three days later, Hibs lost 2–1 again, but this time to Partick Thistle at Firhill. The team worked hard but lacked inspiration and came up against Alan Rough at his best. Things turned a bit ugly in the main stand when a group of visiting fans called for Turnbull's head. The following day, Tom Hart gave the manager his backing.

High-flying Morton, second in the table and playing some wonderful football, came to Edinburgh next, but Hibs peppered the Morton goal with fine efforts, eventually emerging with a creditable 1–1 draw. But soon after, they crashed out of the League Cup with another 2–1 defeat to part-time Kilmarnock. Increasingly desperate, Hibs failed to lure ex-Ayr United and Leeds United goalie Davie Stewart from West Brom with a £70,000 move. The team soon lost again: 2–0 at Tannadice after another spineless display.

At the end of the first quarter of the league campaign, Hibs were rooted at the bottom with just three points from nine games. Their goals-scored record – a measly nine – was the poorest of all thirty-eight teams in Scotland. Next, they travelled to play a Rangers team who were having major problems of their own and were stuck in the bottom half of the table. Even so, the wise bookies of Glasgow only offered 7–1 on Hibs winning. Predictably, they got it right and after Jackie McNamara was sent off harshly after 35 minutes, Hibs went on to lose 2–0. Those in the know were soon confiding to reporters that relegation would cost the club £120,000.

On 27 October, Bobby Hutchinson scored Hibs' first goal in three games against Aberdeen with a brilliant header, and for long

Bobby Hutchinson. *Copyright unknown*

spells the 7,000 crowd at Easter Road thought Hibs would hold on for a vital win; then Andy Watson – a future coach at Hibernian – popped up with a last-minute equaliser. It felt like a defeat. Even when Hibs were playing well, things were going wrong. A week later, Hibs went ahead one minute into the crucial relegation clash at Dens Park from an Ally MacLeod penalty, after he had been tripped in the box. They held the lead till half-time but ended up losing 2–1 thanks to goals by Millar and Fletcher for Dundee. The Hibs defence was woeful and the team as a whole seemed incapable of winning games that were there for the taking. To add further insult, the *Evening News*'s Stewart Brown tells readers that Dundee were just 'an aimless team with little more than honest endeavour'. Yet they ended up winning easily. One win in twelve league games made it official – Hibs were now in crisis.

* * *

Just two days after the Dundee defeat, the saga of Best at Hibs kicked off when Stewart Brown devoted his entire back-page column to the idea that Hibs should move for the star. Brown's argument was simple: Hibs required a famous personality to lift the club in their time of need and there was no bigger celebrity in the game than George Best. Tom Hart obviously agreed and soon phoned Fulham manager Bobby Campbell to ask for permission to speak to the Northern Irishman. (Despite having played in America recently, George was still registered as a Fulham player.) The next day, Hart had a brief telephone chat with Best, who showed an encouraging level of interest in Hibs' proposition.

The wider reaction to the deal was one of disbelief, and not just among supporters. The *Daily Record* got it spectacularly wrong with a story saying that Best had turned down Hibs, claiming that the he 'just laughed' when Bobby Campbell told him of the offer. The west coast media in general thought the idea was a joke, but that only made Hart more determined to prove them wrong. Across in the east, Stewart Brown followed up his original scoop with the story that Fulham had given the go-ahead for Hibs to open negotiations with Best.

Ian Wood, who had joined *The Scotsman* in 1954, was as sceptical as every other reporter when the story broke, but knew that his colleague in the North Bridge office had a habit of being right.

'Stewart Brown was a good colleague to work with and he was also a very fine journalist. He was a very knowledgeable man about European football at a time when it wasn't really fashionable to take an interest in these things. He was very close with a lot of the top European managers and he always knew the league standings on the continent; which team were doing what over there. He was always aware of how strong international sides like Belgium were back in the 1970s, when other journalists were quite dismissive of them. Stewart was also very close with Tom Hart and with Eddie Turnbull, whom he knew from his days as a player. Working for the local evening paper, Stewart was always well tucked in with both of them; they used to go to Stewart rather than the morning papers.

Stewart must have acted as a bit of a go-between for Hart and Turnbull when they did deals like the one that brought the two Norwegians (Refvik and Mathisen) to Easter Road the season before.' Brown certainly had helped the Hibs hierarchy in the past – indeed when Hibs signed Alan Gordon from Dundee United, the *Evening News* man assisted in setting up the deal.

Eddie Turnbull told reporters that Best might just be interested in what Hibs had to offer, even if they were rooted at the bottom of the league. In reality, Turnbull was not happy that Hart and Best had been talking behind his back and that the chairman guaranteed that the Northern Irishman would play whenever possible. Turnbull later confessed that he should have quit there and then when his control over team matters had been challenged so blatantly. Against his better judgement he stayed on, but his relationship with Hart went downhill fast following George's arrival. Whatever his private thoughts, Turnbull maintained a positive line with the press about George's presence throughout his stay at Easter Road. In all the coverage I came across, there was not one negative comment from Turnbull, and all the players I spoke to remember the manager telling them how lucky they were to have George on board.

With Turnbull now in the loop, the club had further telephone talks with Angie Best while the man himself was in Belfast on business. Cynics were already circling, pointing out that Best had been on television just a few days previously saying he would play for nothing for any English Division One team and take any wages at the end of the season when he had proved his worth. Despite rumours of interest from Ipswich Town, there were no takers and George was left twiddling his thumbs while living in Southend with his wife's family. But 11 weeks after their last league win, Hibs were ready to take the gamble. Ian Wood told his readers how George might just be the player to capitalise on the undoubted skills and promise within the Hibs squad. 'It's a lack of belief in themselves that is Hibs' main problem. They could be doing with a bit of swagger. If George Best can supply some – and Eddie Turnbull is convinced he can – then by all means let's be having him before it gets any later.'

George, Angie and Tom Hart at Easter Road. *Scran*

A potentially dull home game against Kilmarnock on 10 November suddenly became the centre of attention throughout Britain, as George and Angie Best arrived at Easter Road. Mrs Best, who was dressed immaculately and sporting designer shades and knee-high boots, looked slightly out of place amid the grey tenements of Albion Road. Passers-by – including a young Charlie Reid of The Proclaimers – stopped and stared at the incongruous site as Tom Hart guided the couple through the throng of reporters and photographers. Considering that he hadn't played football for some time, George still looked remarkably trim, though he did have that trademark slightly sheepish look on his face of a boy just about to indulge in some mischief. As the couple entered the main stand five minutes prior to kick-off, spontaneous applause broke out among the stunned faithful. At half-time, George walked onto the pitch to help Lawrie Reilly draw the winning tickets for the new Hibs Goldliner lottery. By a weird twist of fate, they picked out Best's

George and Lawrie Reilly. *SNS Pix*

ticket, winning the Northern Irishman £1. After the match, Tom Hart told the press that George had left a message on his answering machine intimating that he would be interested in making the trip north. On the morning of the Killie game, Hart had met the Bests at the airport and whisked them off for lunch at 'his office', the Queensferry Hotel, where the Hibs board held their meetings every Friday. As they discussed terms, George made the right impression by ordering an orange juice while everyone else sipped champagne.

George gets an idea of the task in hand. *Scran*

On the pitch the Hibs players – obviously aware of a genuine football legend looking on – played well and Ally MacLeod scored an early goal to raise spirits even higher. The striker played a delightful one-two with Ally Brazil before stroking the ball with ease into the net. But late on in the second half, there was a characteristic capitulation and Killie's George Maxwell brought everyone back down to earth with a late equaliser, latching on to a punched clearance from Hibs keeper McArthur, who had previously bravely defied the Killie attacks. The Easter Road faithful were eventually grateful to take a point and hope that better days were just around the corner. Undaunted, Tom Hart told the press that the Northern Irishman was the type of player who could revitalise the team overnight and also give Scottish football a shot in the arm. Best told reporters that until he was convinced of his own match fitness, he would not be commenting on Hibs other than to say he was impressed by the city and the club – the players having apparently given him a 'warm and sincere' welcome. No doubt the generous offer from Hibs, which chairman Tom Hart reckoned could not be bettered by any other British club, helped to concentrate the mind of the heavily indebted star. The *Daily Express* cartoonist McCormick summed up the mood of disbelief among the nation when he drew two Hibs fans walking past a placard announcing 'Best to sign for Hibs'. One fan says to the other: 'That would soon put a stop to his happy-go-lucky, fun-loving, carefree outlook on life.'

CHAPTER FOUR

GEORGE SIGNS FOR HIBS

On 13 November, Hart and Turnbull flew to London then took a chauffeured limousine to watch Best perform at a testimonial match for Ipswich Town manager Bobby Robson. At much the same time as the Hibs duo were driving to East Anglia, George was also travelling on the same road to his date with destiny. Angie asked George en route if he was nervous. His answer was an emphatic 'no'; instead, he felt a sense of real anticipation to be playing back in a country where the game really meant something – in comparison, American soccer seemed tame and artificial. He had also just read a press article where Jimmy Greaves told how much he regretted retiring early from the game. Surprisingly, considering that he hadn't played a competitive game since leaving America in July, George stole the show and the mercurial Northern Irishman must have impressed the Edinburgh delegation as he sprayed passes left and right with unerring accuracy and laid on a goal for Alan Brazil. Hart was no doubt equally taken by George's pulling power – the attendance of 24,000 was 8,000 more than for Ipswich's previous home match. When George arrived at Portman Road, film crews jostled to get near him; cameras flashed, microphones were thrust into his face and a battery of questions fired at him. One excited man held a young boy above his head and yelled: 'there son, now you can say you've seen the great George Best'. Hart must have been hearing cash registers ring above the bedlam.

The game ended in a 2–2 draw between Ipswich and an English XI: the England side had taken a two-goal lead through Kevin Reeves and Glen Hoddle, only for Paul Mariner and Brazil to haul the Tractor Boys level. As he left the pitch, the fans rose in unison to applaud and chant George's name. The only worry for the visiting Hibees was that George picked up an ankle knock in a clash with Ricky Villa. The following day, Best had to call off a meeting with the Hibs men and go for treatment, but by then the deal was more or less done.

The fact that George Best was back on the market was being noted elsewhere and there was talk of a £90,000 offer being tabled by a Greek First Division side. Ipswich also offered him an extended trial period. But George let it be known that he was just about ready to sign up for a spell in Leith. 'If Hibs can negotiate my transfer from Fulham, then I am prepared to play in Scotland. They came up with an offer that is different . . . in cash terms it is unbelievable, but I want to make sure I am fit . . . I am much fitter than I thought I was but I am 33 now and the legs do not respond as they did when I began 18 years ago. Experience can compensate for that failing, especially if I have plenty of young fellows around me.' He reckoned that after only ten days' training, he was now about 70 per cent of the way towards full fitness. Fed up with the gypsy lifestyle he had led for the past four years, he even held out the prospect of staying in Edinburgh longer than a year: 'Who knows, I might like it so much up there that I shall stay.'

The following day, the *Daily Record*, working hard to make up for being scooped, published a photo of a topless George and Angie with the Northern Irishman's torso strategically placed to – just – protect his wife's modesty. Fulham manager Bobby Campbell consulted his board and the transfer to Hibs got the green light. George went with the London club's best wishes, but Fulham's deputy chairman, Brian Dalton, later gave the game away when he confided: 'I would have willingly carried him up the M1 to Scotland on my back after all the heartache and trouble he has caused us.'

So just over a week after breaking the story, a front-page headline in the *Evening News* screamed 'Best Signs'. The deal was for one year and to secure George's services, Hibs shelled out £50,000 to Fulham plus 15 per cent VAT, which included payment of a £10,000 loan that the London club had made to Best. Without the repayment of the loan, Fulham would have pulled the plug on the deal. If George was to be subsequently transferred to another club for more than £50,000, Fulham stood to get 70 per cent of the difference, and Hibs 30 per cent. Part of the deal was that if Hibs won four games in a row when Best was playing, he would receive a £5,000 bonus. George agreed to play a minimum of 12 games for Hibs, though – ominously – there was no written agreement between club and player, just a handshake between Hart and Best. George posed for a photo of him putting pen to a paper at Craven

George signs on. *Press Association*

Cottage, watched by Eddie Turnbull and the Fulham club secretary, George Noyce. Manager Eddie Turnbull claimed to be 'absolutely delighted' by the signing, telling the press: 'the way he looks, he could go on playing for years . . . we needed a new face and could not have chosen a better one'. *The Scotsman* called the signing of Best a 'little miracle' and argued that – even at 33 – Best's talents would make a considerable impact in a league where world-class players were a bit thin on the ground. James Lawton of the *Daily Express* also welcomed the move, recalling George's drinking habits which made the last days of the Roman Empire seem like tea at the vicarage. Lawton believed that Best had finally grown up – albeit too late to have any meaningful impact on recapturing his glory days. George reinforced this by telling the newspaper: 'So much has gone wrong in my life. But it's never too late to save something. People come up to my wife and say, "look after him won't you", as though I am some waif on the street. Sure I've made mistakes, but you're a fool if you do not learn from them.'

Almost immediately, rumours began to fly as to how much Hibs were paying George per game. The common consensus back then was £2,000, but George himself put the figure at £2,500 when he wrote his first autobiography in 1982. Either way, it was a hell of a lot more – as much as 20 times – than his new teammates were earning and pretty soon there were rumours of disquiet among the players. (When he eventually started playing for Hibs, the stories began that one star player who was jealous of George was not passing the ball to him. But as one fan told me: 'That all changed when George pinged the ball over the guy's right shoulder for him to score. George Best was the guy's best buddy after that!') In these days of astronomical salaries, it's hard to take seriously the pay-packets of the Hibs stars of 1979–80. Even the £2,500 per game which George earned seems chicken feed now. But to shine a little perspective on the issue, Best's salary was twice that of Peter Shilton, who was reputed to be one of the highest-paid footballers in England at the time.

The wages disparity was a cause of real disquiet among the Hibs players, who had a reputation for being the most militant members of the players' union, with Jackie 'The Red' McNamara and union rep Tony Higgins to the fore. The players soon demanded a meeting with Tom Hart, who placated them by agreeing to double their win bonuses until the end of the season. Club captain George Stewart was also approached by other players to raise the cash issue, and made a visit to Turnbull's office. He was sent off with a flea in his ear. Turnbull told him: 'Away you go. That Jackie the Red and that MacLeod are winding you up about Best's wages.' But Eddie Turnbull can't have been happy either, as Best's wage put the

manager's own salary in the shade. (Tom Hart later pulled one of
the rebels aside before George's home debut, took him out to the
front of the tunnel, pointed at the massive crowd and told him, 'see
son: THAT is why George is getting paid more than you!')

Sensing that the trouble in the ranks could ruin his plans, Tom
Hart went on a charm offensive in the media, telling the *Sunday
Mail* how George's wages were being paid for directly by the Hart
family and so were not a drain on the club's limited resources. 'The
match fee he receives is being paid for by four Hibs fans – Tom
Hart, his wife Sheila, and sons Tom and Alan. I don't own a
racehorse, I don't gamble and I never bought a yacht. Hibs are my
only concern.' Tony Higgins, who now works for FIFPro – the
World Players Union – told me how his basic wage back then was
£110 plus bonuses, but also adds that the players' resentment was
soon quelled by Hart's promise to double their bonus.

Whether Tom Hart paid over the odds is debatable. On a couple
of previous stop-offs, George was paid much less – £300 a game at
Stockport County and £600 a match at Cork Celtic. At Fulham,
Best was paid only £500 a week, but also received a £10,000
signing-on fee and the use of a London apartment and car. Back in
1974, Best had been paid around £11,000 just for turning out four
or five times for a team called Jewish Guild in South Africa. Either
way, hiring a superstar does not come cheap, and George himself
claimed that he could have got ten times the Hibs salary if he had
followed up on offers to play in Saudi Arabia. In his own autobiography, he commented: 'I might sometimes feel disappointed
with myself for prostituting my talent by playing for poor teams
simply to make some easy money, but then, why do good actors
appear in poor films? I was being paid to entertain people and . . . I
could have some fun along the way.' But whatever his wage,
George's status never went to his head. Teammates at Easter Road
soon discovered that the most famous footballer in the world
preferred bacon rolls to the *à la carte* menu at top hotels, and
would return from training in the back of a van rather than travel in
a limo. Personal hygiene was one of his obsessions though (at least
when he was sober) and teammates recalled how he used expensive

George dons his new team's kit for the first time. *Mirrorpix*

fragrances and would spend ages after a game manicuring and caring for his feet with all sorts of exotic powders. Jackie McNamara remembers: 'He was the first footballer I ever saw who carried a bag full of nice-smelling stuff to use after he had a shower. He used to have deodorant which cost £80 a bottle; I remember wee Hutchie [Bobby Hutchinson] used to borrow it off him.' He was also a dapper dresser when sober, although strangely he neglected to take the same care over his footwear – preferring to wear one pair of shoes into the ground before investing in another. However much he was on, money wasn't the sole motivation for George. Bill Barclay, who used to drive George back to his hotel after games, recalls how he once failed to persuade George to travel to two events that would have earned the star an easy £4,000.

George gets to know his teammates. *Scran*

* * *

While George worked on his fitness levels, his new teammates were defeated 3–0 at Parkhead in mid-November. Goals by Lennox, Sullivan and Edvaldson put the Celts on easy street, but errors by McArthur and Brazil made the job a lot easier for the Glasgow outfit. A couple of days later, Northern Ireland manager Danny Blanchflower asked George to use his time at Easter Road to play his way back into the international set up. Best had won the last of his 37 caps two years previously against Holland.

Scotland was by now in the grip of Best-mania and he was soon swamped by more than 300 letters from Hibs fans – 98 per cent wished him well, though he admitted receiving a few sent by 'cranks'. One of Scotland's finest ever footballers, Celtic's Jimmy Johnstone, got in on the debate and argued that the Best signing was the greatest thing to hit Scottish football in years. 'Suddenly there's personality back in the game, someone who is willing to take men on, who wants to take chances on the field, who is not going to be tied down by rigid team plans.'

News of Best's arrival hit Scottish football with what the *Evening News* called 'the force of a hurricane' and the local media were right at the centre of the storm, the giant daily papers in Glasgow, London and Edinburgh vying to get the latest scoop on the great man. The *Daily Record* kicked off the media feeding frenzy with a front-page banner headline: 'Mac-Best', to trumpet what the paper called the most ambitious signing in the Edinburgh club's history. George's better half, Angela, let readers of the *Evening News* into a few secrets of her life with the mercurial footballer. Newly returned from Los Angeles, where she was personal assistant and trainer to the pop star Cher, Angie was gamely trying to rein in the notorious philanderer. 'People are always saying, "What do you think of George's girlfriends?" Well, I knew what he was like. He likes a drink. He's a bit of a lad. That's why I married him. Our relationship is much stronger and it's getting better. George knows that if I'm not happy, I'll leave. He realises that now.' Angie also disclosed that the world's most famous footballer knew his way around a kitchen. 'If George wants a cup of tea, he knows he has to make it himself . . . and I never wash a dish. I've never washed a dish in my life. George knows that, he washes the dishes himself. He's very good about the house. I say, "Stop off and pick up some milk George", and he does. He's very intelligent, a sweetheart of a man.' Angie told how George went for the paper every morning and how the couple spent their spare time going on long runs. Until signing with Hibs, weekends had been spent with George's in-laws in Southend – where George ate fresh prawns and played snooker with his father-in-law. Initially, Angie decided to stay south of the border while her husband travelled north. She told me: 'When he moved up to Scotland first, I stayed behind in England. He didn't want me to go with him, he was a bit embarrassed and wanted to try and do it himself.'

The other half of the couple told the *Daily Record* that he had finished with the birds and the bevvy. And he had a message for those waiting to see him fall flat on his face. 'I don't intend to muck it up this time – I have caught the football bug again. I want to train. I want to show people I can still do it. It annoys me to see players who are not as good as I am playing for First Division clubs. I am off the bevvy . . . I have had it as far as that is concerned. I'm not going around the nightclub scene either, all that supposed glamour just does not appeal to me any longer.' As if to prove the point, he said he had just sold his Manchester nightclub, though he did still have an interest in two bars there.

CHAPTER FIVE

TWO DEBUTS

Love Street on a bleak November day, with its tin-roof enclosure
and crumbling terraces, probably wouldn't have been first choice
for Best to make his debut and indeed Hibs, eager to try to capitalise
on the Best hype, cheekily asked for the game to be switched to
Easter Road. The Saints not surprisingly told them where to get off.
Undeterred, Hibees in their thousands prepared for the trip west,
with Leith-based Curran Coaches having to turn fans away. On a
normal away day, they would have struggled to fill a couple of
coaches. This time, though, they ended up sending 15 45-seat buses
packed with supporters through to Paisley – including one bus
which had been renamed George Best #1! A company spokesman
commented: 'We have had phone calls all week, from as far away as
Hawick and Dunbar, from people we have never heard of before.'
Twenty-four hours before the kick-off, scores of media poured into
Easter Road for a chance to see George train with the rest of the
squad and hear him talk about his hopes for the future.

On the match day, the miserable weather kept the crowd down to
13,670. Still, the attendance was almost three times what St Mirren
could have normally expected, and brought the visitors a cheque for
£5,190 – on their previous visit they got £2,700. The ground's tiny
press box was full of hacks from all over Europe, including some of
Fleet Street's finest who were slumming it for the day in Scotland.
Two dozen photographers congregated at the tunnel for a sight of
the great man in a Hibs strip. Strangely, though, it wasn't George's
first visit to the Paisley ground – he had played there two years
previously for Fulham in the Anglo-Scottish Cup. This time, the
home club put a photo of him in action for Fulham against Wolves'

George training. *Scotsman*

Willie Carr on the front cover of the match programme. Up in the main stand, Tom Hart chain-smoked nervously while Angie, wrapped in a tartan blanket to keep out the Paisley chill, enthusiastically cheered her husband's every touch. Also present was Scotland's Minister of Sport, Alec Fletcher.

The programme cover from George's debut. *Copyright unknown*

The game itself gave George an idea of the task in hand. Despite a promising opening half-hour, Hibs eventually came to grief, with George largely anonymous for much of the first-half and only really coming to life when Hibs were 2–0 down and facing defeat. The Irishman roamed back and forward across the pitch, rarely wasting a pass, although the response of some of his new teammates left a lot to be desired. It was an omen of things to come. St Mirren, who were not a bad side, seemed to be coasting it, with two goals from their highly rated forward, Doug Somner. George netted in the dying minutes with a crisply hit shot past Billy Thompson after waltzing through the home defence. Seconds later, with Hibs facing a 2–1 defeat and with the referee poised to end the game, Best

In action against St Mirren. *Scotsman*

almost pulled off a carbon copy of his first goal, twisting past three men on the edge of the box and firing in a shot which fizzed past the right-hand upright. That was vintage Best and it gave Hibs fans a glimmer of hope for the rest of the season. George walked off the pitch to a standing ovation from the huge travelling support.

First game, first goal. *Scotsman*

The *Daily Record*'s top sports reporter, Alex 'Candid' Cameron, thought that even at 33 and obviously unfit, Best outclassed those around him. Cameron hadn't seen an event like this in Paisley since David Lapsley held aloft the Scottish Cup 20 years previously. *The Scotsman* reported that George gave, 'a controlled, perfectly paced performance in his preferred hunting area between wing and midfield'. But watching from the touchline, Eddie Turnbull's worst

George shadowed by Frank McDougall. *Scotsman*

fears had been confirmed early in the game. 'He found himself in space on the edge of the box, and in days gone by he would have done a lightning-fast shimmy and dispatched the ball into the net. This time, his legs seemed unable to follow what his brain was telling them . . . his legs were gone, and anybody with any nous about football could see it.'* Another Hibs legend, Joe Baker, was more positive and reckoned that Best still had the special magic.

* *Having a Ball*, Eddie Turnbull and Martin Hannan, Mainstream, 2006.

Don Morrison of the *Sunday Mail* was probably the most percep-
tive of the watching reporters when he commented: 'For long
periods of the game, Best reminded me of Jim Baxter when he
tried to make his comeback. The brain was working OK, the skill
was there in abundance, but sadly missing was the physical fitness
required to bring it all together.'

After all the hoopla died down, Hibs were still rooted to the foot
of the table and pointless in games away from home. The squad's
confidence was at an all-time low, with quality players like Mac-
Leod and Callachan erring on simple passes and missing chance
after chance in front of goal. Saints' boss Jim Clunie had a wry smile
on his face after the match, saying: 'I don't mind them having the
star man if my boys get the points'. George complained to reporters
about the harsh treatment meted out by St Mirren defenders, but
vowed not to be kicked out of the game. He also gave an insight into
the pressure he was under by saying that playing at Love Street was
more nerve-racking than appearing at Wembley. (In his pomp, even
when playing in cup finals or league deciders, George never suffered
from pre-match nerves.) He told the press that, 'it's obvious Hibs
aren't getting the breaks, we could have had it won in the first 25
minutes and I'm really sorry that the team didn't win'.

After completing his interviews, George headed to Glasgow
Airport in a chauffeur-driven Daimler and flew south, where he
spent the next few days working on his fitness, playing in a
testimonial for Wrexham skipper Gareth Davis and helping the
Welsh side to a 3–2 win over Wolves. He also took part in a 5-a-side
tournament at Wembley indoor arena. Back in Edinburgh, Hibs
stoked-up the Best-mania by announcing that the expected massive
crowd for the next home game against Partick Thistle would be
entertained before the game and at half-time by the Craigmillar Pipe
Band, the under-18 world champions no less!

* * *

George may have signed on for Mission Impossible, but his task
became just a wee bit more probable with a deserved 2–1 home win

against Partick Thistle on 1 December. Thistle played with nine men in defence for large parts of the scrappy game, but then, they were managed by Bertie Auld, who earned a deal of notoriety for exploiting similar tactics as Hibs manager a few years later. As *The Scotsman*'s Ian Wood recalled, the Jags were a team 'whose flair and adventure in pursuit of points away from home were hardly the subjects of hushed discussion in the taverns'. Ian was crammed into a press box that, once again, was heaving with strangers, including one reporter who had travelled from Denmark to see Best's home debut.

All eyes on George and 'Benny' Brazil. *Scotsman*

George was in fine form, showing delightful touches on the ball and, just before the break, testing Thistle keeper Alan Rough with a long-range free-kick. One 50-yard pass by the Northern Irish star was described as a 'work or art' by Sandy Beveridge of the *Daily Record*. As the half-time whistle blew, Hibs were cheered off the park, already 2–0 up thanks to a penalty by Ally MacLeod and a Brian Whittaker own goal. In the second-half, the Maryhill outfit stepped up the pressure and Hibs keeper McArthur had to save a penalty from McAdam. When Alex O'Hara netted one for Partick

19 minutes from time, it meant sweaty palms all round for Hibs fans. Their heroes held out for the win though – their first in 14 weeks of trying!

When the final tally was made, the official match attendance was 20,622 – far higher than the 12,000 that turned up for the League Cup semi-final between Aberdeen and table-topping Morton at Hampden on the same day. The Easter Road crowd was more than double what would normally have been expected for the fixture, and legend has it that the ground contained a fair sprinkling of Hearts fans eager to see George in action. Craig and Charlie Reid, who would later become The Proclaimers, were on the east terracing, as was another future star. A very young Dougray Scott, who went on to be one of Scotland's finest actors, later recalled: 'To see Best play for any team was incredible, but to see him play for Hibs was a huge thrill and very moving.'*

Hibs' gamble on Best seemed to have paid off, and they disclosed that his first two games had earned the club £18,000 – easily covering George's wages and travelling expenses, with a bit to spare. Even Thistle did well out of the day, travelling home to Glasgow with a cheque for almost £9,000 – a not inconsiderable sum back then. Tom Hart felt even more vindicated in his decision when a few days later reporters voted him McKinlay's Scotch Whisky personality of the month for his efforts in bringing George north of the border. Hart won £100 and a gallon of whisky, which he kindly donated to the squad's end of season party. It was the first time that a chairman had gained the honour and later that month, George and Angie signed one of the bottles, which was auctioned for charity.

After the game, George sipped on a glass of lager and told the press: 'The young lads in the team are nervous. I used to make the same mistakes at their age, my aim is to calm them down and I'm shouting more than I've ever done.' George signed a football to raise cash at an auction to help Cambodian children and with the lager unfinished he headed off into the night and back to the

* *Observer Sports Monthly*, 2 March 2003: 'My team: Hibernian', by Dougray Scott.

Angie and George and a bottle of whisky. *Scotsman*

NB hotel to meet his father and younger brother, both of whom were staying there before flying back to Belfast on the Sunday. The same day saw George fly down south to do his bit again for another worthy pro when he played 90 minutes and scored for a Select XI in a testimonial for Derby County full-back David Nish.

But any hopes Hibs had of maintaining the winning momentum were lost when they found themselves without a game the next weekend because of the League Cup final. Hibs tried to arrange a glamour friendly against Atletico Madrid, but the Spaniards wanted more than £20,000 to play, which was £6,000 more than Hibs were willing to pay. So instead Hibs travelled to Rugby Park, where they lost 4–0 to Kilmarnock. Milo Nizetic, a Yugoslav keeper, made an inauspicious debut for Hibs and George had a quiet game in front of 4,000 fans. Another friendly a couple of days later at Easter Road was much more to his liking, as Hibs cuffed Leicester City 3–2 thanks to an Ally MacLeod hat-trick. Managed by Jock Wallace, the Midlands side was full of Anglo-Scots like ex-Hibees Bobby Smith and Martin Henderson, and also included a young Gary Lineker. Best was on top form in front of a crowd of 6,240, including Scotland manager Jock Stein, who was there to take a look at Leicester's Scots contingent. After 16 minutes, the Northern Irishman rolled back the years with a piece of breathtaking skill, skinning a defender on the edge of the box before back-heeling the ball into the path of MacLeod, who gleefully slammed the ball into the net for the first of his goals. The luckless keeper Nizetic broke his hand and left Scotland for home with his hopes of a contract unfulfilled. After the game, George had a meal with Eddie Turnbull, and the manager found the player to be charming and engaging company. But he later confided that one close-up look at Best's face, which was already starting to show the yellowing side-effects of alcoholism, convinced Turnbull that George still had a drink problem and that his signing would be a disaster for Hibs.

After the Leicester game, many of the players went to a nightclub near Waverley Station and experienced Best-mania for the first time up close. Within a few minutes of entering the club, a posse of press photographers and glamorous local girls surrounded them. Tony

Higgins advised George to leave and he soon did a disappearing act. Indeed, early in his stay in Edinburgh, George was on his best behaviour, restricting himself to a quiet pint of shandy or lemonade when he ventured out. Of course, he hadn't always been so circumspect earlier in his career, and the ever-present danger that he might go off the rails again led the club to appoint the dominating figure of Higgins to keep an eye on the Northern Irishman. Bill Barclay, who sat in on some of the after-game sessions in the old supporters club, says: 'George was great company, but you never really got a minute with him, people were coming over all the time and trying to speak to him, offering him drink.'

George toys with a Thistle defender. *Scotsman*

The BBC invited George to appear on their upcoming Hogmanay show, although there is no record of him taking up the offer. But Best's arrival in Scotland didn't impress everyone. The Reverend George Grubb of Craigbank Corstorphine Church did his best

I. M. Jolly impression by telling the press: 'I cannot see for the life of me that any footballer is worth that amount of money, especially when you consider the surgeon and the nurse who work long hours and never hit the headlines and will not be paid anything like that in their working lives.'

CHAPTER SIX

OFF THE WAGON

Just when it all seemed to be going so well, George proved the doubters right and went AWOL on 15 December. The previous week he had posed for the *Daily Record* in a kilt worn back-to-front, which was perhaps an omen of the problems that lay ahead.

George in a back-to-front kilt. *Mirrorpix*

All was going to plan when Angie dropped him at Heathrow, but somewhere before check-in he decided to fly to Manchester instead of Edinburgh. Three days later, he arrived in Glasgow in a car with some old friends from Manchester on the morning of a game against Morton, looking tired and emotional. Tom Hart sensed how the press might react if George didn't go to the game and asked the star to at least sit on the bench. Best replied politely: 'I could try to sit on the bench Mr Hart, but I might fall off.'

In his absence, Hibs lost 2–0 at Cappielow to Morton in what was a desperate game played out on a dreadful pitch, with Scotland's answer to the great man, Andy Ritchie (aka The Idle Idol) taking the spotlight with a superb first goal. Derick Rodier had the difficult task of replacing Best for Hibs but did well and could have scored before the home side took the lead. To put the seal on a miserable day, goalie Jim McArthur was struck in the eye by an object thrown from the crowd and was lucky to avoid serious injury.

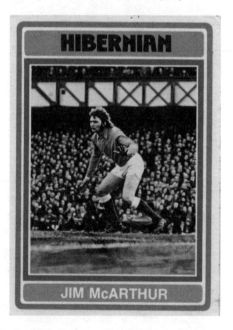

Jim McArthur. *Copyright unknown*

George's no-show, together with news that he had also failed to turn up for a testimonial earlier in the week for Norwich's Billy Steele sparked rumours that the star had fallen off the wagon, and the Scottish press fell over each other in the rush to say: 'I told you so.' The *Daily Record*'s Alex Cameron told readers that the Northern Irishman had let the fans down. 'When a footballer, even a superstar like Best, turns up in a Rolls Royce, having clearly been parted from a razor during this morning, it does raise some interesting questions.' The official line from the club was that Tom Hart had given George the OK to attend a long-standing dinner appointment in Manchester on the night prior to the game and when he turned up at Glasgow's Central Hotel on the day he was declared unfit because of knee and ankle injuries. But the truth gradually emerged in the following weeks. Best attended the function without the club's permission and when he arrived the next day, Hibs covered up by saying he had an injury. He had, in fact, been on a three-day binge and despite apologising and thanking Hibs for covering up his behaviour, he hadn't learned any lessons. Once he had made his peace with Hibs, he took a fast black taxi to the airport and headed south on the next plane to take up where he'd left off, leaving Hibs to head for the Morton game minus their talisman. When he had sobered up, George tried to play the part of the sinned against rather than the sinner when he told *The Sunday Mirror*: 'I turned up and they were willing to let me play. It would have been easy to fake an injury after 15 minutes. I could not do it, fans had paid to see George Best, and they weren't going to see me cheating.' There spoke an alcoholic still in denial.

The question on every fan's lips was why had he had gone off the rails when everything seemed to be going so well? Many years later, George explained his capacity to self-destruct by saying that alcoholics don't live life logically; instead, they operate on impulse or drunken instinct. Once a drinking session started for George, it had to run its course – irrespective of the feelings of those who loved him or those who relied upon him. And in George's case the binge usually had to take place away from his home. He once told a reporter that he was not a vodka-on-the-cornflakes drunk. 'When

Angie and I moved into our rented flat in Putney, we stocked a bar with £200 of drink. I swear the cork hasn't come off a bottle.' Angie herself told me how she could sense one of the drink binges coming from afar. 'George suffered from depression, he would be fine for a while and then the depression would take over. He would start sleeping in late, not showering, not shaving and eating high sugar content foods. I believe that in Britain we do not understand the dangers of a blood sugar imbalance. George couldn't help himself as the depression started to take over and he would just go off to some dark place in his head and alcohol was his only escape.'

Tom Hart and the rest of those at Hibs who had gone out of their way to help George shouldn't have felt slighted. George wasn't singling them out for any reason – indeed, he had let many people down in a similar fashion before and would do it regularly again later in his life.

Just a week after missing the Morton game, though, George was back in Edinburgh and – in a scenario that would become familiar in the next few months – all was forgiven. He arrived in Edinburgh, met up with club officials for a meal and was photographed the next day getting heat treatment for his 'injuries', after doing 100-yard sprints under the watchful eye of Eddie Turnbull. George issued strenuous denials of all the rumours that he had been on the lash during his absence from Edinburgh. 'I am bloody sick of my name being dragged through the mud every time I don't play a game.'

That same day, the local papers carried advertisements where George rather incongruously modelled suits for local tailor Tom Martin. But there were more important things on the horizon – in the shape of a vital home game against Rangers; the first time in his career that George was to face the Glasgow giants. The night before the game, George had to head out to the airport to pick up Angie off her London flight. Cabbie John McBain collected him from outside the North British Hotel only to discover that it was a return hire. John recalls how he had arranged earlier to take his parents to a Christmas dance at the Maybury, the famous Art Deco roadhouse and diner out near the airport at 7 p.m.:

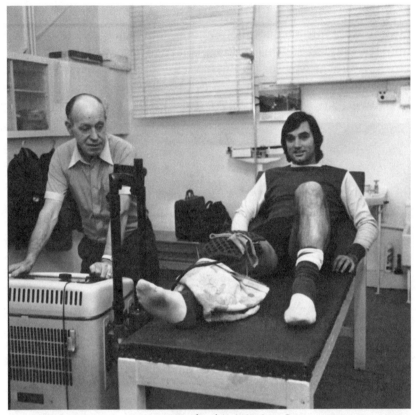

Best gets treatment for his injuries. *Scotsman*

'Well now I had a problem! I was going to have to do a return journey, which would make me very late to pick up my parents. George and I were having a chat about football and Hibs were playing Rangers the following day, he was fine and so I eventually plucked up enough courage to mention my predicament. Would he mind if I stopped on the way to pick them up and drop them off on the way to the airport. "No problem," he said, so I knocked on my parents' door and told them I had a surprise in the taxi. My dad was a great Hearts man, however he was over the moon to meet George and he autographed my parents' dance tickets, which were later raffled off for charity.

'So after I dropped my parents off, it was out to the airport. George went into the terminal building, but was back out in a few minutes only to say his wife's plane had never taken off from Heathrow, as it was snowbound. Well I didn't know what to say, but he just laughed and said, "back to the hotel please". What a gentleman he was. He even gave me a tip at the end of it all.'

Best shows Rangers how it's done. *SNS Pix*

On the day of the Rangers match, 18,740 turned their back on the pre-Christmas shopping and braved freezing temperatures to see the game. They made the right decision, as Hibs came out tops 2–1 in a torrid game. Before the match got underway, Tom Hart accepted his £100 cheque for winning personality of the month. Tommy MacLean put the Gers ahead after 37 minutes, but George inspired a classic comeback, playing a key role in both Hibs' goals.

George delights the home fans at Easter Road as he puts in his best performance for Hibs against Rangers.

Tony Higgins got the equaliser – one of the contenders for goal of the season – but later paid tribute to George's pass that set up the chance. The Northern Irish star delivered an exquisite 40-yard pass to Ally MacLeod, who set up Higgins, and Tony still believes that George's performance on the day was his best in a Hibs strip. George ran the show, one of the few players to master the tricky underfoot conditions, and constantly showed his teammates what to do and where to play. He even had a hand in the winner. When George took a quick throw-in out on the right, Higgins arrowed in a cross, Colin Campbell headed the winner and the Easter Road men were cheered off the pitch by their fans at full-time. The game, though, was punctuated by personal vendettas, with elbows and boots flying – in the end it was a surprise that only four players were booked.

Rangers' manager John Greig later said that the flint-hard, frozen pitch made the game a lottery, but the visiting team's keeper George Young saved three fine efforts from Best; two left-foot shots and a free-kick. Best was sometimes guilty of dwelling on the ball too long and occasionally drifted out of the game, but overall he was the star of the show. After the game he said the narrow margin of victory was a 'complete travesty'. He told reporters how the mood in the dressing room had changed for the better – now there was no shortage of noise and banter in comparison to the morgue-like air a month previously. 'The atmosphere in the dressing room at half-time was unbelievable . . . it was the noisiest I have ever known . . . we knew we were the better team in the first half and were angry to be 1–0 down at half-time.'

As ever in these games, the atmosphere between supporters had been poisonous. At half-time, police with Alsatian dogs had to move into the no-go area between the two sets of fans as bottles and cans flew overhead. Hundreds of Rangers fans had found their way into the Hibs supporters' end, several fans were injured and 18 supporters arrested inside and outside the ground. Tom Hart later tried to shift some of the blame onto Hearts fans who had headed for Easter Road after their own match against Dunfermline was cancelled. Maybe, but Hibs and Rangers fans never need any encouragement to kick lumps out of each other, and they were still arguing and shouting abuse at each other at full-time as the Easter Road DJ played 'Auld Lang Syne'! But George did his bit to defuse the crowd trouble during the match by playing up to his reputation as a boozer. As trouble flared at the away end, a can of beer flew out of the crowd and landed at his feet as he prepared to take a corner. Best picked the can up and with nearly 20,000 pairs of eyes trained on him, he feigned to take a swig from the can. His actions momentarily stopped the aggro and the ground rang to the sound of laughter and applause from both sets of fans. After the game, he tried the real thing with a couple of pints in the 50 Club among admiring Hibs fans.

George attended the Hibs team's Christmas party in the Persevere Bar at the foot of Easter Road and was on his best behaviour, taking time to sign countless autographs. He spent Christmas Day with the in-laws in Southend, but the trip nearly ended in disaster when he went for a five-mile run and a nail pierced the sole of his training shoe. His foot was gashed, but not badly enough to cause any long-term problems. Angie told me how the festive period was a worrying time for her and her husband. 'I remember being in Edinburgh on New Year's Eve and we were both standing staring out of our hotel window at 10 p.m. and I was thinking "is he going to snap, is he going to go for a drink?" But he was good that night and on New Year's Day he turned up on time to play for Hibs.' Ironically, all George's best efforts came to naught, as the home match against Dundee scheduled for 1 January was postponed because of the poor weather.

CHAPTER SEVEN

SUSPENDED

You'd be a hard-pressed to call it a bandwagon, but whatever impetus Hibs were building up after the wins against Partick Thistle and Rangers was soon floored by the Scottish weather. The scheduled game at Pittodrie against Aberdeen on 29 December was called off because of a frozen pitch, and a similar bone-hard surface also meant the postponement of the game against Dundee at Easter Road. The latter call-off came despite the best efforts of groundsman Alex Kerr and a collection of volunteers who had left the comfort of the Supporters' Association bar to lay straw on the pitch. The letters page of the *Daily Record* offered evidence that George hadn't won over all the sceptics. Reader G. Rogers of Wishaw wrote: 'Since his introduction to Scottish soccer he has bombarded the media with expressions of self-pity and a portrayal of himself as a national martyr . . . grow up, belt up and play up!' Mr Rogers won £10 for his efforts.

Hibs arrived at Rugby Park on 5 January to meet Kilmarnock for the sixth time that season including friendlies* and had yet to beat the Ayrshire outfit. That miserable run continued with a soul-sapping 3–1 defeat. Ex-Aberdeen man Bobby Street scored a superb hat-trick; his first was a goal that Best in his heyday would not have disowned. Standing with his back to goal, Street collected a cross from Houston and beat the defence with a magnificent overhead kick that seemed to defy gravity. Two–nil down at the break, Hibs

---

* George was well aware that the small number of teams in the top league was leading to boredom among fans and during his time in Scotland he regularly used his newspaper columns to call for a bigger league, along with a season to run between March and November.

emerged and gathered in the centre circle, where George gave the team some tactical advice. The upshot was that Hibs began to play with more patience and control and Colin Campbell scored a consolation for them ten minutes from time. But the final score didn't reflect the balance of play, indeed Hibs squandered lots of good chances, one journalist even went as far as to say that they had just given their finest display since the previous season's cup final. Ally MacLeod should have had a hat-trick and even missed from the penalty spot, sending his shot banging off keeper McCulloch's right-hand post. A crowd of 6,000 was treated to an hour-long masterclass from Best as he excelled with fine distribution, including a trademark 50-yard pinpoint pass, and even had a late shot cleared off the line by Paul Clarke. The *Glasgow Herald*'s David Belcher's abiding memory of the game was of George, 'standing rain-sodden with hands on hips in the centre circle in the game's final minutes surveying the ruins of another Hibs defeat'. After the game, George showed his compassionate side again by agreeing to donate one of his Northern Ireland strips to help raise money for handicapped kids. The defeat and results elsewhere meant that Hibs now had the worst away record of all 130 Scots and English sides: ten games on the road, no points and only four goals. Home and away they had only managed 18 goals in 19 games.

One week later, Celtic were in town. Despite their common choice in shirt colours and shared Irish heritage, there is actually a fierce rivalry between Celtic and Hibs, and George seemed to revel in the big game atmosphere, turning in a scintillating performance to rival his showing against the other half of the Old Firm the previous month. He looked lean and fit – the sharpest he'd been since arriving in Scotland. After seven minutes Roy Aitken felled him and Hibs won a penalty, but Ally MacLeod hit the bar with his effort. When Tony Higgins missed a sitter inside the six-yard box it didn't look like it would be Hibs' day but, after 26 minutes, George lit up the near 22,000 crowd with a pearl of a right-foot strike from distance that left Peter Latchford clawing helplessly at the ball. Drifting in from the wide and taking a ball from Colin Campbell, who had made an incisive run into the box, Best leathered his shot past the keeper. The goal can still be seen on *YouTube*, complete with expert commentary from Arthur Montford, and in slow motion you can see Best's perfect poise as he rolled back the years to fire in the shot. Not bad considering it was struck with the foot he usually used for standing on! The ground echoed to the cry of 'Georgie Best!' But sadly Hibs could not hold on to the lead in a thrill-a-minute game and after 36 minutes Roy Aitken nodded in an

Jackie McNamara congratulates Best. *Mirrorpix*

equaliser. George was chosen as man of the match, but his skill levels only served to highlight the deficiencies of those around him, even good players like Ally Macleod were toiling, the striker contriving to miss his third penalty in five attempts. 'It's not as if we are missing the penalties by yards . . . Ally hit the bar and the ball came down on the line. Maybe we should campaign to get the goals stretched a little wider. It's crazy and makes me angry that Hibs are bottom of the league and yet can play so well,' said Best after the match. Celtic impressed the Northern Irishman, who called them the best team he had faced north of the border, and in particular he praised winger Davie Provan, whose positive running and dangerous crossing were a feature of the game.

Best hypnotises the ball while John Lambie looks on, suitably impressed.
Mirrorpix

The result suggested that Hibs were in a false position in the league – but Stewart Brown of the *Evening News* laid none of the blame at George's feet. He was quite simply, 'head and shoulders above every player on the park and could have graced any ground in Britain . . . the jeers from the Celtic end were music to his ears'. The *Glasgow Herald*'s Jim Reynolds wondered at the star's razor-sharp mind and his educated feet. 'The figure is a bit more portly and the legs do not respond as readily, but the football brain is still working to full capacity and the fans are loving every minute of it.' The *Sunday People* even deigned to send a reporter up to Scotland for the game, and he was suitably impressed. 'The amazing George Best took on the champions of Scotland yesterday and almost beat them single-handed.' The *Sunday Mail*'s Allan Herron was equally amazed: 'George Best was a role model for every player on the field and every kid on the terracing with his careful use of the ball, close control and short, snappy runs.' The paper carried out a voxpop after the game and, bizarrely, interviewed the comedienne Elaine C. Smith, who was then a drama teacher in the capital. Despite being a Celtic fan, Elaine showed good taste by picking George as man of the match, enjoying his 'glimpses of genius'. Eddie Turnbull concurred. 'He can do anything with the ball and it's a sheer joy to watch him at work. If only he had joined us a month earlier. The man is worth the admission money on his own. We are prepared to fight as well as entertain.' The aggregate attendance for the last three games at Easter Road now totalled an impressive 61,540.

Four days later, Hibs finally won an away game – albeit the match was a friendly. The success came at a snow-covered Filbert Street with a 2–0 win over Leicester City, who eventually went on to win the English Division Two title that year. Jackie McNamara scored his first goal after three years at the club and Tony Higgins converted the second. The club also let it be known that for the remainder of the season, George Best would take the penalties. But the winter weather ensured another free Saturday for Best and his teammates the following weekend. With the Easter Road pitch resembling concrete, the referee called off the game against St Mirren. George had been in town since Tuesday and undoubtedly this latest cancellation must have added to his frustration. He later told the writer Joe Lovejoy that at times: 'It was hard for me to take it seriously . . . I had no friends up there, and I didn't really mix with the players because I wasn't with them often enough to get to know them. After training we would go and have a couple of drinks, but then they would go home to their families, and I was stuck on my own at night in the hotel. There were times when I'd disappear down to London for some company, but old Tom, the chairman, understood. He was a lovely man.' No doubt George did feel lonely and there were times when he opted for Tramp in London instead of a night out at the Persevere Bar in Leith. But he did actually socialise quite a bit with his Hibs teammates and once visited Ralph Callachan and his wife Anne in Corstorphine. Sometimes those more intimate evenings were preferable to a night on the town when George became the most sought after man in the capital, pestered wherever he went by old grannies and younger females. He sometimes teamed up with Jim McArthur and Bobby Hutchinson to go out on the town. The trio became known as the Three Amigos, although as Jackie McNamara says: 'Bobby and Jim were amigos with anyone who had a flat!'

* * *

With Scottish football in cold storage, the newspaper reporters started to look around for alternative stories and were soon asking if George could be about to represent Scotland? It sounded far-fetched, but the papers were full of talk that he was about to play for the Scottish League team in two games – one in Northern Ireland and one in Dublin – in March. Predictably, though, the plans come to nothing, even although George went on the record to say he would love to play for Scotland. The *Daily Express* went so far as to write an editorial in favour of the move. Not everyone was convinced, though, and reader James Robinson of Oxgangs Avenue, Edinburgh slammed the plan: 'No doubt the next suggestion from you or your sports writers will be that Best should receive the freedom of Edinburgh or should be included in the Honours List!'

A little bit of Hollywood at Turnhouse Airport. *Courtesy of Angie Best*

On 25 January, Best flew into Edinburgh via Prestwick airport after spending three days with his family in Belfast, sorting out some business commitments during the trip and also keeping fit by training in his home town. The following day he played in a 1–0 victory over Meadowbank Thistle at Tynecastle (the Scottish Cup tie had been moved from Meadowbank's ground for safety reasons). Hibs were boosted by the return of big George Stewart after a three-month injury absence, but the team relapsed badly into the fearful form of early season. Ralph Callachan scored the winner, but George was far and away the best player on the field, although even he wasn't on top form. Only 8,415 watched the spectacle and George later revealed how difficult it was to raise his game in front of such meagre crowds, saying how he would much rather play Rangers every week. 'Everybody expects you to do so well, but it really is difficult when the other team has absolutely nothing to lose.'

Off the field, Hibs were trying to lure one of the Famous Five, Willie Ormond, to become an assistant to Turnbull at Easter Road. Ormond, who had just recently been given the heave as Hearts manager, declined the offer. The following week, the game against Partick Thistle at Firhill was called off after six inches of snow fell on the pitch overnight. But George was never far from the headlines even when he wasn't playing. He let it be known that he was interested in becoming player-manager of Northern Ireland – the post being vacant since the departure of Danny Blanchflower. In the article in the *Daily Express*, he sounded like a plausible candidate for the job. But within a week the same man would be front-page news in the same paper – under the banner headline: 'My Shame!' and telling readers: 'I am utterly ashamed of myself and deserve everything that is coming to me.' His dreams of graduating to management would have to be placed on hold for a while, as George was about to go off the rails again in spectacular fashion.

A 3–2 win over Morton at Easter Road on 9 February was overshadowed by the banner headlines on the front page of the *Evening News*: 'BEST SUSPENDED'. Once again, Stewart Brown was the man with the exclusive story, telling readers how the Northern Irishman had reneged on an agreement with Tom Hart to train with his colleagues prior to the game. He was given permission to catch a late flight on Friday afternoon because of his need to attend to 'business commitments' in London prior to flying north. George left his London home to head to the airport but somewhere en route to the shuttle flight he had a change of heart. He made no attempt to phone the club and instead went missing before eventually emerging in a London nightclub at 3 a.m. – 12 hours before he was due to play against Morton more than 300 miles away. There was some anger at Easter Road, especially considering how well he had been treated and also because he had earned more than £20,000 in his short time at the club. Eddie Turnbull phoned Tom Hart and asked: 'Where's your man Best?' The chairman was clueless as to his charge's whereabouts until he saw a newspaper picture of George out on the town in London.

Angie, who had boosted Hibs' hopes of a permanent deal by intimating that she fancied living full-time in Edinburgh, did her best to protect her husband from the press, telling the *Evening News*: 'George is not feeling well. He has a rotten cold. He has been in bed for two days and the doctor has been to see him. I have spoken to Mr Hart and told him that – he knows very well.' Told of George's suspension, Angie replied: 'They can't do that.' For the rest of the day, no one was answering the phone in the Bests' Putney flat. When she was next quoted in the Sunday newspapers, the truth was beginning to trickle out. George had in fact being going through one of his 'silly' periods and she was furious at his stupid actions. She later called it: 'A George Best special.' It was the second time in a matter of weeks that he had failed to turn up for a game against Morton. Maybe he just had something against the Greenock club. In any case, his teammates did OK without him, with Ally MacLeod netting a double in heavy rain that kept the crowd down to a measly 5,401. Man-of-the match Willie Murray, who had the unenviable task of replacing Best, also scored with a great header. Jim McArthur, a part-time PT teacher, pulled off a magnificent late save to safeguard the win. Afterwards, Turnbull was full of praise

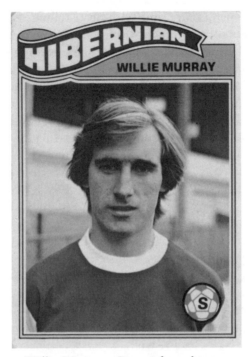

Willie Murray. *Copyright unknown*

for the team: 'Morton were outplayed in the first half and we might have scored four or five.'

George – to his credit – soon issued an apology and offered no excuses for his behaviour. After a high-noon lunch with the player, Tom Hart accepted this personal act of contrition, but other than issue a ban on his charge appearing in any more testimonials (Best was due to appear in a match in honour of Chelsea's John Dempsey at Stamford Bridge) there did not seem to have been any move to try to tackle the root cause of the problem: the player's alcoholism. Hart told the press: 'In the past, George has tended to run away from situations like this so I am delighted he took the first opportunity to come and see me and admit that he was wrong . . . he has to spend more of his time with Hibs and less on his promotional activities.' Hart wanted Best to visit hospitals and supporters' groups and to spend more time with his teammates rather than out raving. 'I expect some of them will invite him up to their homes or out for a jar.' (Unfortunately, some of the Hibs players opted for the latter option.) George agreed to remain in Edinburgh for the next fortnight, and returned to his five-star city centre hotel to prepare himself for a potentially tricky Scottish cup tie against an Ayr United side that had only lost one of their previous 16 games.

Chapter Eight

Sacked

St Valentine's Day in Edinburgh found George holed-up in the NB Hotel, but it might as well have been the dog house. The man who once had to employ secretaries to deal with sacks of letters from fans received only one Valentine's Day card. He didn't send any either, having apparently forgotten what day it was. Maybe the lack of cards triggered something in George's head, because he was soon in the mood to press the self-destruct button again. After a hard training session, he joined his teammates for a few pints in the Jinglin' Geordie. But this time, for George at least, things went too far. When the final round was bought in the Jinglin', the rest of the players headed home to their wives and girlfriends, but George didn't have that option and, alone in the big city, he embarked on a drinking binge that lasted almost five days and very nearly called time on his career at Hibs.

Ordinarily, George could have talked his way out of trouble and told his bosses that stories about his drinking were all exaggeration and rumour. Unfortunately for him, the session in the Jinglin' was immortalised by a photographer's snap of the bleary-eyed star surrounded by a table of empty glasses. The exact circumstances of how and why the infamous photo was taken has long since been clouded by poor memory – not surprisingly given the amount of empty pint glasses on display.

The official party line at the time among the seven or eight players who were present was that they were sober and had sat down at a table where a group of thirsty press men had just finished their standard liquid lunch. None of the bar staff in the busy pub had managed to clean the table and as a result, there were empty glasses

George bleary eyed. *Prosport*

everywhere. According to this sanitised version, while Ally Mac-
Leod was up at the bar getting the first round, a photographer
sneaked into their company and took the shot. When they were
later hauled over the coals, the players told Hibs that they had all
been sober when the photo was taken. Unfortunately, their version
fails to explain how George looks quite so wrecked in the photo.
Tony Higgins told me that the snap was taken by a freelance
photographer who used to hang about with the players at training
and asked to come along for the drinks session. Tony says he tried
to warn George that the heady cocktail of drinks, a superstar and a
member of Her Majesty's press were not a good mix. But George
decided to stick around and soon the inevitable happened. Jackie
McNamara's take on the whole affair is slightly different, he
believes that Bobby Hutchinson started taking photos when the
snapper had gone to the toilet.

Perhaps the definitive version of what happened that day,
though, came from the two men who were there to do an interview
with George. Photographer Tommy Hindley and writer Helge
Åmotsbakken were in Edinburgh to do a feature on George for
the Norwegian magazine *Vi –Menn* (not, as has been written
elsewhere, *World Soccer*). Both men's recollections of the day
can be found in the second half of this book. Whatever the
circumstances, the photo lay unseen for almost a week before
surfacing in the *Daily Mirror* the following Tuesday and was
subsequently seen around the world.

Whoever's memory is right; the irony is that Eddie Turnbull was
well aware of what was going on in the pub that day. The boss was
quite happy to let the players wind down after a tough training
session with a few drinks – believing that it helped team bonding.
Indeed, Jackie McNamara remembers that the gaffer used the
promise of a drinking session as a tool to spur them on through
training. But Turnbull was far too experienced a man to totally turn
a blind eye. A spy in the camp had been phoning him to keep him
informed of the ongoing party, but he refused to intervene, arguing
that the only person who could stop George drinking was George
himself. The manager also reckoned that, as it was Tom Hart who

had gambled on signing an alcoholic, then it should be the chairman who cleaned up the mess once the inevitable happened.

For the third time in just two months, George went AWOL and carried on drinking, despite the fact that a crucial Scottish Cup tie against Ayr United was looming on the Sunday (the game was moved from the Saturday to try to boost the attendance rather than compete with Scotland's rugby clash against France.) Throughout the booze marathon, George hardly ate a bite of food and lost almost half a stone in weight. The only token nod to the notion of keeping fit for the big game was his bizarre decision to switch from drinking vodka to champagne and orange juice because it, 'sounded a healthier option'. On a damp, misty Friday afternoon, he woke in his overheated hotel room: hung-over, lonely and depressed. He tried to beat the boredom by gazing out of the window or by watching horse racing on the television, occasionally flicking channels, for the company of the voices.

In his autobiography, he painted a desperately sad portrait of a 'lonely mixed-up' man who couldn't decide what he wanted from life. He longed for company but inevitably that would mean running the gauntlet of autograph hunters, starry-eyed fans wanting to talk or shake his hand, or even worse dodge the insults from strangers and barflies. 'So I stayed in my room until, as the night drew in, the telephone brought the invitations, the drinks and the company that were preferable to the solitude. Everyone, it seemed, was happy to drink with George Best, and who was I to disappoint them?' The drinking session carried on and by the weekend he was in no fit state to keep appointments. He had been due to train for an hour with the other players on the Saturday, meet Tom Hart for lunch, watch the Hearts versus Stirling Albion cup tie at Tynecastle and then spend the evening with the chairman. He never turned up for the training and was posted missing all day, preferring instead to prop up the bar.

On the Saturday, Scotland beat France 22–14 at Murrayfield, with Andy Irvine scoring 16 points – two tries, two penalties and a conversion – to lead a storming comeback. Meanwhile, across town George Best was limbering up for a night out.

Early on Saturday evening, he was spotted drinking Buck's Fizz (orange juice and champagne) with a journalist friend in the American Bar of the North British Hotel. At 5 p.m., he took a call from his wife and the telephone conversation ended with him slamming down the receiver and returning to the bar. Twenty minutes later, Best's father phoned and shortly after taking the call, the Northern Irishman left the bar and headed off into the Edinburgh night. Workers from the NB Hotel were sent around bars to try and find him and at 5.30 p.m., he was spotted by a fan in a nearby bar, where he stayed for at least two hours. He eventually returned to the hotel and adjourned to the bar where, by chance, he met another group of sportsmen out on the lash: the downcast French team had made their way back from Murrayfield and were in the mood to drown their sorrows. When they converged on the hotel bar, Jean-Pierre Rives, the French flanker, spotted George and invited him over for a drink. Players and fans soon joined together in a party later described by George as 'bedlam'. Local legend has it that Blondie's Debbie Harry was present at the party. Unfortunately, she completed her British tour three weeks earlier and the idea that she would hang around in Leith for the Ayr United game seems a bit far-fetched. But even without Blondie, what followed was a booze-up of legendary proportions that would lead to Best being sacked by Hibs.

As George later recalled: 'That was it. The next thing I know it's Sunday and Hibernian have come to pick me up to take me to the game. The trainer took one look at me and said, "You can't play today, can you?" I told him I couldn't and that was that. I can't remember much about the night before, not even if I got to bed, but I know Rives could drink as well as he played. They all could. And they could hold it as well.'

Around 10 a.m. on Sunday, Tom Hart phoned the hotel to ensure that George was woken up. He was told by a waiter, who was paid to keep the chairman informed, that George had been on the booze all night. The porter couldn't get into the star's room, which was double-locked. Hart called Turnbull, but the manager was adamant that Best was not his problem and that Hibs send two of the training staff along to the hotel. A couple of hours later, the Hibs squad started arriving at the hotel for their pre-match meal. Hibs skipper George Stewart, along with Hart and club director Tommy Younger, again failed to gain entry to the room – George apparently telling the bosses that he would be with them when he was finished entertaining the young lady he was with. Jackie McNamara recalls: 'There were four or five of us came through from Glasgow and we went up to the NB for our pre-match meal and started hearing all these whispers that George had been seen steaming and had been taken up to his bed.'

Here, like the infamous photo story, everything gets a bit confused. Some people will tell you that they remember the trainers John Fraser and John Lambie carrying a legless Best through the hotel. Others insist that when the club officials gained entry to the room, they found George in bed with a glamorous blonde decked out in exotic underwear. George turned to the officials and said: 'what would you rather do, spend the afternoon with her or play Ayr United?' Some people will even tell you that the mystery girl wasn't just a production-line blonde but a very famous American. When I put the mystery blonde's name to Angie Best, she told me her husband had never met the woman. 'I am still constantly surprised by the stories that I hear about what he supposedly got up to when we were together that I know nothing about. What used to happen with George is that he would always look for some way to deflect things away from him. He did that kind of thing up until he died really – I suppose that is what alcoholics do, they are very good at making sure that they do not have to take responsibility. He never spoke to me about this woman – and he used to tell me everything.'

Another friend who knew the star well told me: 'I used to hear George tell a version of that story where a number of other women are mentioned – as often as not a Miss World. Variations of that story were always his response when people told him that he had wasted his life away.'

When he sobered up, George was given the message, 'pack your bags and don't come back' by Hibs. Tom Hart had feared that the rugby weekend – akin to a three-day whisky Olympics – would have been far too tempting and had wanted George to move to a quieter hotel away from the city centre, or to stay with the Harts at their own home. 'Instead, the little so-and-so got to bed at seven in the morning on the day of the game,' Hart revealed.

Over at Easter Road, an above average attendance was eagerly anticipating the game against Ayr, many of them there just to see Best perform. So when the Northern Irishman's name wasn't on the team list, his replacement Willie Murray had to listen to a chorus of boos as his name was called out. Up in the radio box, Bill Barclay was forced by Tom Hart to read out a prepared statement: 'Hibs FC apologise but George Best will not be playing today.' Once the catcalls died down, the game got underway and almost forgotten among all subsequent press hysteria was the fact that the hapless Hibs side had cast aside their dismal league form and embarked on a cup run. They toiled to an unimpressive 2–0 victory over Ayr United. Duncan Lambie getting his first goal for the club and Ally MacLeod scoring the second. Young Willie Murray who had replaced Best played well, despite being booed throughout the game by fans angry at not seeing their hero. After the full-time whistle, Tom Hart summoned the press to the gymnasium under the main stand and told them in grave tones that the marriage between Hibs and Best was over and that the divorce papers had been filed that morning. The sombre mood was lightened somewhat when the chairman managed to stumble over the crate of whisky that he had been awarded only a few months previously for bringing the errant star to Scotland. While all this was going on, George was working off his hangover and was driven to the airport by a reporter, apparently to leave Edinburgh for the last time.

CHAPTER NINE

'THE TROUBLE WITH GEORGE IS . . .'

His career in ruins, George retreated to London, where Angie was threatening to leave him after his latest relapse. From daybreak on Sunday, the press were camped outside his Putney flat demanding answers from the fallen star. The *Daily Express* had a head start on its rivals because of George's regular Monday column in the paper and when the paper tracked him down, he gave a front-page exclusive with the headline: 'Drink is my problem.' George had met the reporter Jim MacLean in the lounge of an Edinburgh hotel before heading off for London. Looking red-eyed but immaculately dressed and sipping black coffee, he said: 'I must get a grip of myself, I am in a terrible mess. What a disaster. My wife and even my father in Belfast have been on the phone giving me hell. I thought I had beaten it. But boredom being in a hotel got the better of me. I just let myself go.' The news that only non-league Workington had enquired about signing him following his sacking by Hibs presumably helped sober him up. Fulham boss Ernie Clay took pity on his old charge, though, and went out of his way to offer George the use of the club training ground.

Back in Scotland, the newspapers were full of the story, with the common consensus being that the Ulsterman's fall from the wagon was a tragedy. *The Glasgow Herald* scooped all its rivals with an exclusive chat with the star, where he partly blamed fans who insisted on buying him a drink. 'They think they are doing me a favour, but they are not. I suppose I should refuse but it's very difficult. Some of them then get offended, they think they own you.

I went up to Scotland last Sunday and I was all right on Wednesday. That's when it all started again. I wasn't quite drinking 24 hours a day but it was pretty well non-stop. Eating and sleeping went haywire. It isn't really fair on the other players and the people who are paying the money. My wife Angie is the one who suffers more than anyone because of all this. It hurts other people more than me – Angela, her parents and my own family back in Northern Ireland. I know other football players going through the same thing, like Jimmy Greaves, and he has got over it. Without wanting to sound big-headed, it's because I have become a personality more than a player. I sometimes go out alone for a few drinks but it never finishes up like that. People are buying them and sending them over and before you know where you are you have too many.' In an unusual aside, he told *The Herald* that he was considering taking up writing and had a few plot ideas for a novel. Everyone seemed to have an opinion on George's condition, with even his old landlady from his teenage years in Manchester, Mary Fullaway, giving her tuppence-worth. 'He seemed fine and very happy when I last saw him. I cannot understand what has happened. He has a lovely wife and if anyone can keep him in line, she can. The trouble with George is that he is too nice, he could never say no – whether it's for a drink or to someone who invited him to open a fête.'

A spokesman for Alcoholics Anonymous issued a solemn message to George: 'You are not alone. There are many famous people in the same situation . . . I know what this boy is going through. He is feeling tremendously lonely and is full of remorse and guilt. It's tragic. But it need not be the end. Many famous people get hooked on drink because they are lonely.' The *Evening News* calculated that the latest sacking would cost George around £40,000 in lost wages between then and the end of the season. They added presciently, however, that, 'money does not seem to enter into his thoughts when he goes off the rails'. Tom Hart commented that the star, whom he had obviously taken a liking to, needed treatment quickly. 'He has a chronic illness and will need to go into a nursing home. I've discussed this with him and he knows what should be done.' To rub salt into George's wounds, it emerged that Northern

Ireland manager Billy Bingham had attended the Ayr game with a view to selecting Best for the upcoming World Cup qualifying game against Israel in Tel Aviv. (The Northern Irish manager eventually gave up on George and omitted him from a squad that excelled in getting through to the second round of the World Cup before losing 4–1 to France. So George missed out on one of the few ambitions he had left in football – to represent his country at a major competition – and we all missed out on seeing one of the world's greatest ever players compete on the same stage as the likes of Zico and Maradona). Strangely, the star's relapse also put paid to a possible career in the movies. The William Hickey column in the *Daily Express* revealed that George was being considered for a part in the prisoner-of-war epic *Escape to Victory*, which featured a host of football stars including Pele, Bobby Moore and John Wark. The columnist added, 'personally, I think he should be given a permanent job at Tramp, the London nightclub. The old place doesn't seem the same without him sitting on his habitual stool at the bar.'

At their wits' end, the Bests were suddenly offered a ray of hope from a most unusual source when a telegram arrived from a group named Conservation of Manpower. The one-line message – 'We can help you' – had a simplicity that appealed to George, who in his periods of painful remorse was always eager to try to find solutions for his ongoing alcohol addiction. Encouraged by his wife, he agreed to seek help from the group, which was made up of dedicated doctors and clergymen, led by Boris Serebro, who helped people battling alcoholism. On the Tuesday after being sacked by Hibs, they met Serebro at his office in St Swithin's Lane, where George discussed the possibility of using Antabuse tablets that would make him violently ill if he took alcohol again. They also talked about the possibility of George receiving oxygen treatment to help battle the depression that was thought to be triggering his drinking bouts.

For a while, the organisation seemed to offer genuine hope for George. They only charged him a token fee and there was no input from psychiatrists. Best seemed unwilling to countenance that his problems may have been psychological, once telling a reporter:

'Shrinks I don't need – my brain is fine and I am sharper than most guys in the football business.' The organisation's office was beside a cake shop and at the end of each therapy session, George treated himself to a chocolate éclair, by way of reward. Encouraged by the group, he seemed confident that he could beat the addiction and also decided to set his thoughts down on record so that he could begin to write his first autobiography. He even felt strong enough to appear on ITV's *On the Ball* programme, saying that Jimmy Greaves' drinking habits – two bottles of spirits a day – would 'only be a starter' for him and blaming directors at Hibs for taking him for lunch over a bottle of wine. 'Maybe it would have been better if they had left me alone. I walk into a room and 60 people want to buy me a drink. I am not alone either – a lot of footballers have the same problem but are afraid to admit it.'

Thirty years on, Angie Best's memories of the Conservation of Manpower group are understandably sketchy, but she did tell me: 'I remember going with George to see this man in London to talk about George's drinking and this man [possibly Boris] said to me, "your husband will always drink alcohol". I was so gobsmacked and hurt by what he said that I just got up from my chair and ran out of the room crying. He had said something that I just did not want to hear. And that's my only memory of the Conservation of Manpower. Anyway, it didn't do George much good, but then again nothing really worked for George.' Sadly, that also included the much-vaunted Antabuse, which back in the dark days of February 1980, seemed to offer just a glimmer of hope to the couple. Angie remembers that even such a dangerous drug as Antabuse did little to deter the dedicated alcoholic. 'After he left Edinburgh, I know that George used Antabuse during his time playing for the San Jose Earthquakes. He went off to a facility near where we stayed in San Jose and he was given the Antabuse to use at home. Every morning before he went training, I would hand him his tablet and a drink and afterwards he would stick out his tongue to show me that he had swallowed it. And that night when he came home, I would find the Antabuse tablet in the pocket of his jeans! This would go on and on and I would say to him: 'George, why do you go through with this scenario when you are not going to take the tablet? And why do you leave it in your pocket unless you want to get caught?' So he wanted me to know he was not taking it, yet he persisted in going through the same scenario every morning.

'I remember another time when he was supposed to be taking the Antabuse and he went on a golf game with his teammates at the San Jose Earthquakes. He came back from the golf absolutely legless and I asked him how he could do it when he was taking the Antabuse and he said: "I just drink through it." He would get all these palpitations and his face would go red but he would just carry on drinking.'

* * *

Meanwhile back at Easter Road, Peter Cormack, who had left Hibs for Nottingham Forest back in 1970 for £80,000, re-signed for the club. The 33-year-old had just been given a free transfer by Bristol City and despite a five-figure offer to play in the USA for Tulsa Roughnecks, Peter moved home. Part of his new remit was to coach the youngsters every afternoon. Tom Hart continued briefly to take out his anger on George – banning him from playing in a match to honour the installation of new floodlights at Chatham Town in Kent. Ex-Newcastle United striker Malcolm Macdonald and former QPR favourite Terry Mancini were also due to play in the friendly. Chatham's chairman received a telegram from the Football Association threatening them with extinction if Best played. It was made plain to the wayward star that Hibs still held his registration, even if they had given him the boot. Testimonial appearances would not be allowed from then on.

Officially on the transfer list, the prospect of returning to America was growing increasingly attractive for the Bests. The unpleasant reality of his condition led Angie to call a halt to their efforts to start a family, and after a modelling assignment at Old Trafford she told reporters: 'Before his latest problem, we were trying to start a family but now I am frightened to take the risk. It would not be fair on children at the moment. I want to cool the situation for a while.' In the meantime, she said she had the star 'on a leash' and would not let him near a bottle of booze. Best had been given the choice between Angie and the booze and had chosen the former – for now at least. 'I don't know why he does it; everything had been going so well – now he's blown it. He does not need drying out. He never drinks at home; he is what is called a bout alcoholic. He drinks when he cannot cope socially and needs to learn why he does it . . . I'll cut off his legs and put him in a circus if he lets me down again.' Angie blamed people in Edinburgh for tempting George to fall off the wagon and she tearfully pleaded with fans who met George not to buy him drinks in the future. 'If people sent him home when he walks into a bar instead of buying him a drink, they'd be doing him a much bigger favour.'

The following week, Tom Hart did a major interview in the *Evening News* revealing for the first time how he had tried to cover up the true reason for George's non-appearance for the two games against Morton. But having overcome his initial anger, the chairman was now leaving the door open for George to return to Edinburgh. 'It is entirely up to George Best whether he plays again . . . the way is clear for him to return. If he flies to Edinburgh any Wednesday night, accompanied by his wife, and trains for the next two days, it will be up to manager Eddie Turnbull to decide whether Best is fit enough to play for Hibs.' Hart revealed that when George had started his five-day binge prior to the Ayr game, he had asked Angie to fly up immediately but she had refused, saying her husband had to stand on his own two feet. Attempts to bring over George's dad and other members of the Belfast family to keep the player company also fell through. Hart thought Best could play for another three seasons if he looked after himself, and Hibs were prepared to help by offering him one more chance. The club were willing to find a flat for the Bests – an offer described by George as 'wonderful and generous'. Hart concluded by asking the media to treat George 'like any other footballer'. There wasn't much chance of that.

On the same day as Hart gave his interview Hibs, without George, sank to a 1–0 defeat against Dundee United at Tannadice.

Willie Pettigrew scored the only goal, although in truth only a fine performance by Jim McArthur kept the score respectable. The result was a real body blow, as United were the closest team to Hibs in the relegation mire. There was now an ominous seven-point gap between Hibs and safety.

CHAPTER TEN

ONE LAST CHANCE

The sad fact was that at his age and with his reputation for unreliability, George really didn't have that many options left to him and it came as no surprise when he accepted Tom Hart's offer. The press reaction to Hart's change of mind was generally positive, in truth they could not get enough of George and the excitement he generated. Jim MacLean in the *Daily Express* called the move a 'marvellous and sensitive act of faith in George and his problems'. George arrived back in Edinburgh for Wednesday training with the rest of the squad as they prepared for a trip to Ibrox. Despite the chairman's plea to give George some privacy, the media were out in force and a battery of cameramen staked out Edinburgh Airport for his arrival with Angie. He gave the reporters what they wanted by proclaiming: 'I've been having private treatment for my problems and I feel that I'm winning the battle.' He was then whisked away by club secretary Cecil Graham for some lunch. When he walked back into the stadium, his team-mates gave out a loud welcoming cheer. George entered into the spirit of things by shouting: 'I'm cured. I'm cured.' Later, at training near the McEwan's Brewery, which gave off a powerful smell of beer, some of the players yelled: 'Hey boss, fetch a clothes peg for Bestie's nose!' George was photographed shaking hands with his fellow players, including new arrival Peter Cormack, and also Willie Ormond, who had agreed to work as manager's assistant. Ormond first joined Hibs in 1946 and stayed there for 15 years before playing his last game for the club in Rome in 1961. In the boardroom, Hibs' AGM heard that the club had made profits of £97,605.

George and Peter Cormack (right) signing autographs. *Mirrorpix*

By an uncanny coincidence, the hot new film at the Edinburgh Odeon on the weekend of George's return was *Yesterday's Hero*, starring Ian McShane as a washed-up footballer who had blown his career on booze and birds. Based on a Jackie Collins book, the film's star, McShane, even bore a close resemblance to George, and as an added twist McShane's own father had once played for Manchester United. Meanwhile, George and Angie moved the length of Princes Street to stay in the Caledonian Hotel under the assumed name of Mr and Mrs Smith. Reception staff were under strict orders only to allow visitors up to the room if they asked for the assumed name and some callers had to go outside and contact George from a phone kiosk before they gained entry. On the night of his return to Edinburgh, George featured on the ITV documentary *Just for Today* about another fallen idol, Jimmy Greaves. George told viewers of the programme, which was narrated by the comedian Peter Cook, himself a talented man with a debilitating drink problem, how tricky it was to come to terms with falling out of the limelight: 'A lot of players look for an alternative, and unfortunately in a lot of cases it turns out to be drink.'

George, alias 'Mr Smith', outside the Caledonian Hotel. *Scran*

On 1 March, Best made his first appearance for Hibs since the Meadowbank game five weeks previously, and his every touch at Ibrox was greeted with a chorus of boos from some of the home support. The *Daily Record*, never a paper to underplay the importance of a 90–minute football match, called the game the most important in Hibs' history and reckoned that many in the near 30,000 crowd were there especially to see George play. He did well, but was eventually substituted early in the second half and replaced by Tony Higgins. George obviously wasn't used to getting hooked and there was a short delay before he was eventually persuaded that he was the one being substituted. It was later explained to the press that George had been suffering from body rashes and sickness, side effects of the treatment he was receiving for his alcoholism. George commented: 'I had to come off because I was feeling so ill; partly because of the treatment I was having for a stomach upset but also because I was in such a terrible condition after all the alcohol. But I knew there was no way I could not play because of the happenings of the previous week and the big crowd expected at Ibrox.'

Despite his protestations, George, it seems, was in fact drunk during his short spell on the pitch. To give him his due, it was a rare occurrence – despite his addiction, George despised the idea of cheating the fans by playing while under the influence. But, as Jackie McNamara recalls: 'That was the only time playing with George that I was aware that he was drunk during a game . . . it was quite evident.' Angie told me: 'I had loads of those mornings when he was in no fit state to play but I had to get him out of bed, dressed and to the game whether he wanted to or not. It was a case of a bucket of water over his face and telling him, "get up, you are going!"'

After Best's substitution, Hibs actually perked up and showed some fire and fury but Rangers – with Ian Redford, a Scottish record £210,000 signing from Dundee, on display – eased to a 1–0 win thanks to a Derek Johnstone goal. Elsewhere, a draw in the Dundee derby meant that the gap at the foot of the table was now a worrying eight points.

The Bests spent the following week looking at flats to rent in

Edinburgh. Hibs were more than willing to help, and offered a flat the club had bought to house two Norwegian players – Refvik and Mathisen – the previous season. But that option, and a cottage outside town, proved to be unsuitable. The Bests, used to the fast pace of London and California, wanted something more central. They eventually ended up living in a smart first-floor apartment at 52 Palmerston Place in the city centre. Ian McDonald, who worked in an office across the street, remembers Angie taking the couple's dog for walks in the private Douglas Gardens nearby. Ian recalls eyeing the footballer, stone-cold sober and bored, whiling away time alone in his flat. 'I could see him, hour after hour, throwing darts at a dartboard. He looked a lonely man. Also, he used to park his car on double yellows at Rothesay Terrace and I remember a friend of mine taking a photo of his car being booked by a warden.' For a while, the Bests had a guest in their spare room as Graeme Wright moved in to help ghostwrite George's memoirs. Graeme spent most afternoons interviewing the star, and the resulting book makes for good reading.*

On the field, things were not getting much better for George and he was hooked again during the Scottish Cup tie away to Berwick Rangers – a move that the *Daily Record* believed put his whole Hibs career in doubt. George, whose effectiveness was blunted by a heavy first-half tackle by Berwick's Henderson, later admitted that Turnbull had taken him off because, 'I wasn't doing him, the team or myself any favours.' But his pride was undoubtedly hurt by the substitution, and he told readers of his *Daily Express* column: 'I was stunned to find myself left behind in the dressing room for the second half of our Scottish Cup tie at Berwick. It was a shattering experience and I am still absolutely flabbergasted . . . it leads to wild speculation at a time when I want to be left alone

* Graeme told me that, some time later when George had returned from America, he asked the writer if he would help him pen some detective stories he had in his head. Pressure of work meant that Graeme turned down the offer, but he still ponders if the project would have worked out. 'George was an intelligent guy and I sometimes wonder if anything would have come of it, something to rival Ian Rankin maybe? But I doubt it.'

to get on with the job at Hibs. I certainly was not the worst player on the park.'

Indeed a lot of commentators, including Brian Scott of the *Daily Mail*, thought that George was one of the better players on the park. When the Northern Irishman failed to appear after half-time, the local fans showed a touching interest in his health. Journalist and long-suffering Berwick Rangers fan Jack Mathieson remembers: 'The fact that Best was in the Hibs team created a lot of excitement in Berwick – as did the fact that we were in the quarter-finals of the Cup, which doesn't happen that often! I remember some home fans waiting, cameras in hand, to snap him coming off the Hibs team bus. In the event, though, his performance was a bit of a let-down. He struggled to make much impact against a Berwick defence that had earmarked him for special treatment and he was hooked at half-time.

'A social club called the Black & Gold stands a few yards behind the main stand at Shielfield and Best's non-appearance for the second half was greeted by Berwick fans with the song, 'George is in the Black & Gold again, Black & Gold again, Black & Gold again', in tribute to his legendary drinking habits.'

Berwick – managed by Dave Smith who played with George for Los Angeles Aztecs – almost snatched victory late on when Stuart Romaines hit the bar, but the dull match ended in a 0–0 draw in front of a crowd of 7,278 (receipts of £8,766). Most of the action worth noting took place off the pitch when a wooden perimeter barrier collapsed in the Hibs section 20 minutes into the game. Scores of fans spilled onto the speedway track that surrounds the pitch and the match had to be halted for a couple of minutes as several supporters were helped away for treatment. Tom Hart later slammed the performance of his team, saying, 'some individuals were a disgrace to the Hibs jersey . . . this sort of show will not be tolerated'. Hibs fans consoled themselves with the news that Hearts were cuffed 6–1 by Rangers at Ibrox on the same afternoon.

The replay saw another lifeless show by Hibs, but at least they managed to grind out a result, an Ally MacLeod goal giving them a squeaky 1–0 win over the wee Rangers. But the game was a grim, painful slog for the crowd of 9,500 to watch, Hibs showed no confidence or direction and they were jeered off the park at the final whistle. Best missed the game due to a groin strain picked up in training.

The following day, Hibs signed Bobby Torrance from St Mirren for £30,000. A trainee quantity surveyor, six-foot-tall Torrance, twenty-one, had already scored seven goals in seventeen appearances for the Paisley outfit that season. Torrance was effectively a replacement for Tony Higgins, who left after eight years at Easter Road to sign for Partick Thistle for £25,000. He had scored eight goals in over thirty games for Hibs that season and his departure was difficult to fathom. Higgins, always a shade more eloquent than the average footballer, went on to become boss of the players' union in Scotland and is now a regular on the after-dinner speaking circuit.

The rest of the squad soldiered on and travelled up to Dens Park for a crucial tussle with Dundee. Best's presence was still a cue for mild hysteria among the locals, with police having to clear autograph hunters off the pitch before kick-off. He enjoyed a good game too, using the ball with his customary accuracy and having a headed goal ruled out for offside in 69 minutes. Hibs, in fact, were the dominant side in a desperate struggle and the Edinburgh men had the bulk of possession and chances. All of which made the result – a 3–0 defeat – hard to accept. Torrance, who hit the woodwork, and ex-Hearts youngster Lawrence Tierney made their debuts in the first-team, but a goal by Dennis Corrigan was followed up by late strikes by Shirra and Ferguson as Hibs caved in. To add to the gloom, the following week's game at home against the dreaded Kilmarnock was called off after six inches of snowfall on Edinburgh.

Whatever his faults, George was never afraid of applying himself to rigorous training, and after being welcomed back to Easter Road he soon lost almost a stone in weight. Even away from the ground, he often went jogging with Angie and their dog Dallas on Portobello beach. George would clock up four miles before he even thought of lunch. He and Angie were now settling into Edinburgh life; George even claimed to have been off the booze for almost a

Best arrives for training. *Scotsman*

month and to be feeling the better for it. 'I know I can't drink because if I do, I'll be ill.' But he and his wife had to be vigilant when they headed out for a meal, quizzing waiters to make sure the food did not even contain a trace of alcohol. Angie told the press: 'George daren't even risk a dish cooked in wine. Things such as

Coq au Vin, one of his favourites, are completely out. Half a dozen drinks could kill him.' George was occasionally still going out with some teammates after training, though, to play darts in quaint wee pubs along the Royal Mile, but while they had a pint of lager, George was more circumspect: 'I drink Perrier water and pour it myself – I cannot risk somebody lacing my glass.' Watching other people enjoy an alcoholic drink while he remained sober was not easy, though: 'I desperately envy them their bottle of wine.' When he travelled down to London, he still could not resist the lure of the bright lights, hanging out in Tramp nightclub even although he was on the wagon.

George claimed that he was now more aware of his responsibilities to his wife and to the people at Hibs who had given him so many chances. Being in Scotland seemed to have provided him a more positive attitude to life; he felt close to the people, an emotion he partly attributed to his family's Scottish roots. He had ruled out an immediate return to Florida and declined an offer to play in New York. The plan was to try to get set up with a team in California later in the year, and stick it out in Edinburgh until the end of the season. Angie later recalled: 'We found a lovely little apartment just outside the city and quickly grew to be very fond of our new home town. The locals seemed to accept us, too, which is always important.' Mrs Best was soon modelling again and accepted an invitation to help open a new section of Blair Drummond Safari Park. She was snapped holding a feisty three-month-old lion cub and two five-week-old Canadian black bear cubs. Angie showed a good deal of fortitude by maintaining a beaming smile despite the fact that all three animals decided to relieve themselves on her during the photo shoot. George, meantime, spent some of his spare time driving around Edinburgh in his Turbo Saab listening to Fleetwood Mac. At a set of traffic lights one day, a local newspaper vendor took one look at the handsome footballer with his glamorous wife and snazzy car and delivered the immortal line: 'You must be mad laddie, you threw it all away!'

On 24 March, the SFA hammered the final nail in Hibs' coffin by rejecting the idea of league reconstruction, which would have seen

Angie and the lion cub. *Courtesy of Angie Best*

Hibs and another struggling club avoiding the drop so as to allow a 12-team top tier for the following season. With the club effectively relegated, George wouldn't have been blamed if he'd cut and run for the Californian sun. Instead, he stuck it out and produced a magnificent performance in his next match. Until then, George had reserved his outstanding performances for the big games against the Old Firm. But on a Tuesday night at Easter Road, he turned on the style in an otherwise low-key game against Dundee. After seven minutes, he collected a Colin Campbell pass, shrugged off three tackles and bulleted a tremendous shot just wide. Seven minutes later, he found Willie Murray with a defence splitting 40-yard pass. Jack Adams of the *Daily Record* told readers that it was a pass that the other 21 players could not even think about, never mind pull off. The Dundee defence were chasing shadows and ex-Hibee Eric Schaedler was lucky to stay on the field after he hacked down Best. The Northern Irishman scored the first goal after 24 minutes with a beautifully struck shot from just inside the box. Having picked up a Campbell pass, he ghosted his way across the penalty area before

flashing a drive past a helpless Donaldson. Later, he set up Willie
Murray for the second in a 2–0 victory. But it wasn't just the goals
that really impressed, it was his all-round performance; even when
he faded late on, he was head and shoulders above the rest of the
players. The consensus in the press box was that George's performance had been a sheer joy to watch. Stewart Brown, a veteran
reporter, sounded genuinely amazed by the Northern Irishman's
display, calling it an exquisite entertainment as Best paraded his
bewildering skills. George was at his vintage best: 'an eager,
energetic and raving destroyer'. He laid on five choice chances
with delightful passes, which his colleagues managed to spurn, and
also hit the woodwork. Jack Adams told readers: 'When he is bad
he is very, very bad . . . when he is good, he is still something extra
special. George Best pulled back the curtain of misspent years to
unveil again a talent that has seldom been equalled in British
football.' Eddie Turnbull – no mean player himself – raved about
the performance, saying it was a privilege to see him in action:
'What a player, anyone who hasn't seen this fellow play does not
know what they have missed.' Stuart McLaren, Dundee's tough
defender, called Best's performance brilliant – in a different class.
Dundee's manager, Tommy Gemmell, thought Best was excep-
tional, with his visionary passing as good as ever. Sadly, only
5,019 were there to witness the spectacle. After the game, Hibs
denied rumours that George was set to join New York United to
team up with Rodney Marsh.

Two nights later, Best and Ralph Callachan attended a sports
quiz at Stewart's Melville College. George sipped fresh orange and
lemonade all evening and stole the show, getting nearly all his
questions on football and horse-racing correct. When asked what
his greatest achievement in football was, he showed a good understanding of Hibs' history by replying: 'It's still to come – when Hibs
win the Scottish Cup this season.' He later took time to sign more
than 200 autographs and talked enthusiastically to star-struck
pupils and parents.

But a dispiriting 4–0 defeat to Celtic at Parkhead followed soon
after. George, looking decidedly podgy and wearing a pair of shorts

George scores against Dundee. *Copyright unknown*

that left little to the imagination, displayed some nice passes as Hibs did well in the first-half, and at the break it was 0–0. The home fans, who gave him a rough welcome during the warm-up, actually ended up applauding some of his finer touches. George was pleased with his improving fitness levels, and his ability to go past defenders and deliver pinpoint passes to colleagues, 'if they could read the game properly'. Tommy Burns replaced Jim Casey and Celtic then took control, with Lisbon Lion Bobby Lennox stealing the limelight from George. Soon after the break, Ally Brazil conceded a needless penalty, handling a Roy Aitken cross that was heading out of play. Lennox converted the spot kick and then Frank McGarvey scored his first goal for Celtic since signing from Liverpool earlier that month. Johnny Doyle and Roddy MacDonald completed the rout in front of 22,000 fans. The *Daily Record* ventured that Hibs would now be looking forward to meeting Celtic in the cup semi-final, 'with the enthusiasm of a blind man in a minefield'. Afterwards, Eddie Turnbull said: 'I was happy with the way Hibs played in the first half, when we contained the champions without too much bother. But we lost an unnecessary goal through a penalty kick at the start of the second-half and never recaptured our earlier composure.' The boss revealed that he had also had a long talk with Northern Ireland manager Billy Bingham, who was still keen to get George back into his squad.

George admires Bobby Lennox's skill. *Scotsman*

CHAPTER ELEVEN

RELEGATION

Throughout their season from hell, Hibs could always console themselves that their home form had been not too bad. In fact, going into the clash with Dundee United on 2 April, they hadn't lost at Easter Road for six months. But long before the final whistle, that record was in tatters and the fans were leaving in their droves. Davie Dodds and Willie Pettigrew scored the goals for United, but only a string of fine saves by Jim McArthur managed to keep the score semi-respectable. For the first time since his arrival, George was a big disappointment on the pitch – turning in such an anonymous performance that he barely received a mention in the press reports of the game.

Just three days later, George returned to form, showing some glorious touches, but Hibs lost yet again on the road. This time the venue was Love Street, where George had made his Hibs debut six months previously. St Mirren won 2–0 this time with goals from Logan and Richardson, but only 8,000 were there to witness the defeat – 5,000 less than on Best's debut. By then, the novelty was starting to wear off and attendances were in decline. With only a few games left in the season, Hibs had played fourteen games away from home with no wins and only four goals scored. It was a shocking record, rooted in the fact that once they went a goal down they seemed to automatically lose all of their spirit and fight. In the previous week alone, they had shipped eight goals in the second-half of three games. The only hope of salvaging anything from the season was . . . the Scottish Cup.

Ian Wood of *The Scotsman* once wrote about the relationship between Hibs and the Scottish Cup, telling readers that a long-suffering Hibee once told him, 'that there were times in his youth when he felt as though the best years of his life were being frittered away staring out of dismal railway carriages carrying even more dismal Hibs supporters away from defeats in the Scottish Cup.' In fact, Wood was being charitable; Hibs and the Scottish Cup isn't so much a relationship as a loveless marriage riven by domestic grief. Rival fans – especially those with maroon blood – love to make jokes about Hibs' inability to win the trophy. One Hearts fan even has a website that provides the exact time since Hibs' last triumph – when writing this book, the clock stood at 107 years, 182 days, 4 hours, 1 minute and 50 seconds. Even back in George Best's day, the 1902 win was a very distant memory. So if Best could have engineered a triumph in 1980, he would have become a freeman of Leith overnight. On a more personal level, it was probably going to be his last chance to reach a British cup final. Remarkably, a domestic cup winner's medal always eluded him at Manchester United and indeed his last semi-final appearance on UK soil was in the 1968 European Cup campaign.

So there was a lot riding on the semi-final and the Hibs squad prepared by heading for the East Lothian coastal resort of Gullane, where they played golf and trained in the spring sunshine. Eddie Turnbull slipped away from the hotel on a spying mission and saw Celtic lose 3–0 in a league game at Tannadice. It was a good omen and the feeling was that the Glasgow giants – who would eventually self-destruct and lose the league title race that season to Aberdeen – were already going off the boil. On the day of the semi-final, a crowd of 32,925, including George's younger brother, Ian Busby Best, made their way to the Hampden slopes and the early signs were good for the Hibees, who were 6–1 outsiders with the bookies. Early on in the game Best, who was making his first appearance at the national stadium since he'd helped Northern Ireland beat Scotland 1–0 there in 1971, slipped in a cute pass for Bobby Torrance, but the striker spurned the chance, shooting wide of Peter Latchford's post. Only a couple of minutes later, it was Celtic's turn to have a great chance and this time Bobby Lennox made no mistake. But despite this setback Hibs continued to match'

George jousts with Celtic. *Scotsman*

their rivals and were unlucky not to be level at the break. Gordon
Rae collected a cross from Duncan Lambie, but sent his effort over
the bar from six yards out. George later recalled: 'We missed an
easy chance immediately before the interval and then fell to a sucker
punch early in the second-half. After that it was a minor massacre.'
The fatal second goal came three minutes after the break, when
Jackie McNamara was short with a back pass that was intercepted
by Davie Provan, who tucked the chance away. Jackie later was
wracked with guilt, saying he felt responsible for both Celtic's first
two goals. Thereafter, Celtic strolled to their fortieth Scottish Cup
final with further goals from Doyle in the fifty-fourth minute,
McLeod (80) and McAdam (87). When the final whistle sounded,
the 5–0 result was an embarrassment for Hibs, their biggest ever
defeat in a Scottish Cup semi-final. And they had lost a few semi-
finals – 13 in total. Only Best, who consistently passed the ball well,
and dogged defender George Stewart were judged to have done
themselves justice. The post-match inquests centred on Eddie Turnbull's decision not to play Ally MacLeod and Peter Cormack, but

the reality was that Hibs were coming to the end of their worst season in fifty years and hadn't managed a goal in their last seven games outside Edinburgh. The manager himself called the match an 'utter humiliation', and he was right.

George himself was fairly sanguine about the latest setback – which was his eighth time on the losing side of a cup semi-final. He later commented: 'Major finals, it seems, are just not my thing. Four semi-finals in the FA Cup, two in the League Cup, one in America and now one in Scotland. It makes me wonder how we managed to reach the final of the European Cup. If Hibs had made the final of the Scottish Cup, I'd have stayed behind.' The cold reality that the season was now effectively over hit home and almost immediately it was revealed that George had spoken to Bill Foulkes, his former Old Trafford teammate who was then chief scout at San Jose, about a move stateside in the summer.

The Scottish Cup defeat effectively spelt the end for manager Eddie Turnbull, and on 15 April the club sacked him. The dismissal brought to an end a 25-year association with the club as player, trainer and manager. The defeat to Celtic was the final straw for the club, but in truth Turnbull had been under pressure since back in October when he was booed by some fans following a defeat at Firhill. If anything, George's arrival took some heat off the manager, but a succession of poor results made his sacking almost inevitable. Turnbull was allowed to keep his Audi club car, but was too scunnered to demand a better deal. At the age of 57, he was out of a job and the prospects of a new career seemed slim. The official club line was that his departure was on 'amicable terms'. Turnbull later let the truth be known, but on the day of his departure the only hint of bitterness was when he said that he had been sacked by 'my best friend'. On the subject of Best, Turnbull sounded unequivocal, saying he had no regrets about taking the Northern Irishman to Easter Road. 'He still retains magnificent ability. I hope he continues to please the fans for some years to come.' But his true feelings came out when he wrote his biography a few years back – he felt his sacking had been inevitable from the day George Best walked through the front doors of Easter Road. In the book,

Turnbull blamed lack of investment by the chairman for his demise, along with the decision to bring in 'an alcoholic who disrupted our team and destroyed any chance I might have had of grinding out a survival plan'. To his credit, Turnbull stresses that at his peak, George was a magnificent player and that he had a lot of time for the sober George, whom he found excellent company. He just thought it 'unutterably sad' that Best had allowed his God-given talents to be diluted by the booze.

The day after Turnbull's departure, Willie Ormond signed a two-year contract as manager with the specific remit of getting Hibs back into the Premier League. Ormond – a popular man around Easter Road – promised to add some competitive attitude and hardness to the side. But he was under no illusions about the task in hand. 'That's me back to sleepless nights again,' he told the media. That evening, the Hibs Supporters Association showed their appreciation for Best's efforts by presenting him with an Edinburgh Crystal whisky decanter and glasses. A nice touch, though probably not the most appropriate choice of gift given the circumstances.

The change of manager had an instant effect, as Hibs gained a hard-earned point in a 1–1 draw on a windy night at Pittodrie. It was the first point won after a total of 24 hours of league matches away from home. A dogged defensive display did the trick, with Jim McArthur outstanding in goals and George Stewart and Craig Paterson effectively blunting the dangerous Dons attack. After 64 minutes, Gordon Rae scored from a fine Ally MacLeod pass, but Andy Watson also netted for the Dons. Unfortunately George, for the first time north of the border, got into trouble with the authorities, after being booked for dissent in the second half and having a scuffle with Dons skipper Willie Miller in the tunnel at full-time. Best later attributed the flare-up to Miller's anger at the Hibs team's tactics: on two occasions, the Northern Irishman punted the ball from the half-way line back to keeper McArthur in a bid to avoid losing possession and so protect their precious point. 'I suppose he was upset because we'd held them to a draw, so interfering with their bid to win the Scottish Championship. He said something like, "I thought you were supposed to be able to play a bit", to which I retorted, "yeah, well it's cost you the league", and next thing we're in a bit of a tussle, with the other players pulling us apart.' The incident lasted barely a matter of seconds, but Best and Willie Ormond were later summoned to referee David Murdoch's room, where George was told that he would be reported to the SFA for 'adopting an aggressive approach to another player'. Next day, the papers were full of stories of 'Best's bad-tempered end to his Hibs career'. In his own biography, Willie Miller wrote that George was well past his best and a shadow of his former self. 'Indeed, it was sad to witness him being unable to replicate the skills that had made him one of the most engaging characters to grace a football field.' A crowd of 16,000 was 4,000 more than the Dons' last home game and most of the extra spectators had come to see George, although his performance made Miller vow never to carry on playing past his sell-by date.

Prior to the game against Dundee United on 19 April, most of the press had the impression that the match would be George's swansong in Scottish football. If so, then this was hardly the way to bow out as he shone only intermittently in a 2–0 defeat at Easter Road. Best fired into the side netting after rounding Hamish McAlpine and also had another shot saved by the United keeper. But overall it was poor fare for the Hibs fans – the fact that only 4,921 bothered to turn up spoke volumes about the team's poor form. It also showed that the Best-mania of a few months back was long forgotten. Second-half goals by Willie Pettigrew and Eamonn Bannon were enough to secure United's win – their fourth success against Hibs that season.

The United defeat was the first of seven league games scheduled for Hibs in the space of 17 days. Next up, Bobby Houston bagged a double as Hibs lost yet again to Kilmarnock. Ally MacLeod scored a penalty for Hibs, but a 2–1 defeat was hard to stomach for the paltry crowd of 2,659. George watched on from the commentary box, where comedian Bill Barclay was doing his best to raise the spirits of the faithful. At the end, the Northern Irishman was persuaded to take the microphone and offered a heartfelt thanks to the club and fans for their support during the previous six months. He concluded by saying that he was 'a little sad to be leaving when the team is doing so badly, but I'm sure that with the tradition Hibs have, they will soon be back in the Premier League'. And with that George prepared to jet off to sunnier climes.

George and Bill Barclay. *Scotsman*

Without him, Hibs played their third game in five days as they tried to make up for all those cancellations during the winter. A trip to Firhill ended in a 1–0 defeat, though, as Colin McAdam put Hibs to the sword. As if things could not get any worse, news filtered through that Hearts had won promotion on the same night. The following day, Willie Ormond gave his verdict on what he'd seen so far and wielded the axe, releasing 12 players on free transfers, including Bobby Hutchinson, Colin Campbell, Davie Whyte and David Reid. Three days later, he blooded Musselburgh schoolboy keeper Dave Huggins in a 1–1 draw away to Morton. The Greenock side led through a controversial penalty, but a late Ralph Callachan goal pulled Hibs level and earned them only their second away point of the season. The midfielder had pounced on the loose ball after goalkeeper Roy Baines failed to hold a Peter Cormack shot. That final trip away from Easter Road left Hibs with the lamentable record on the road of played 18, won none, drawn 2 and lost 16. Away from home, they scored only 6 goals and conceded 36.

After saying his goodbyes in Edinburgh, George left Angie in London to tidy up their affairs as he flew out to California. Against her better judgement, Angie had agreed to give it another go together in California in the forlorn hope that the move would help George change his ways. There wasn't much chance of that, unfortunately. Best was met at San Francisco Airport by representatives from his new club and driven the 40 miles to San Jose, where he was due to hold a press conference. Things appeared to be looking up for him again, but with the indefatigable logic of an alcoholic, he decided to give the press conference a miss and instead he headed back to the airport to catch a flight to Los Angeles, where he then embarked on a three-day booze session. When he eventually sobered up and returned home, he played well as his new club San Jose Earthquakes lost 4–2 to Edmonton Drillers, laying on a fine goal for his South African teammate Andries Maseko.

But with a sense of wretched inevitability, George's Californian summer quickly turned sour. The North American Soccer League, in an attempt to nurture local talent, ordered that each team should have eight Americans in their line-up. The result was a sharp decline in standards. As George commented rather unfairly: 'If I thought Hibs were bad, they were world beaters compared to San Jose . . . it was like parks football.' Also, the hard pitches in the USA actually played havoc with his fitness; his knee had to be drained of fluid with a needle three times on match days. He also required cortisone injections for a toe injury, to enable him to play in the Indoor Soccer League.

Back in Edinburgh, Willie Ormond claimed his first win as Hibs boss on 29 April, as the team came from behind to win 2–1 at home to St Mirren. Torrance and Rae scored for Hibs. On the same day, Angie revealed in *Woman's Own* magazine how her errant husband had a poetic soul and occasionally penned verses which helped

Best with Hibs supporters after their game against San Jose Earthquakes in
1981. *Courtesy of Alan Hart.*

placate his wife after one of his alcoholic bouts. The painfully
honest poem would never win any prizes, but it certainly shows a
different, more sensitive side to the Northern Irishman:

> If my desperation leaves us room for hope,
> My hope is that our love will see me through,
> For through that love my mind will clear,
> To reveal our children free of that desperation. I love you.

Angie told the magazine: 'How can you give up on someone who
writes of beautiful things . . . who lies beside me in bed at night and
makes me cry at the beauty of the poetry he has written?' She told
me: 'When he was in a soul-searching mood, he would occasionally
write poetry. George was not your average footballer, he was a very
intelligent man – nobody I've met could do a cryptic crossword
quicker than him! I love it when people get to see that there was
much more to him than being a footballer.'

But although the few months spent together in Edinburgh were relatively happy ones for the couple, who were again making tentative plans to start a family, there was always the danger of George relapsing. Angie told the magazine how her husband went into a major sulk when she suggested a name for the baby that did not meet with his approval. A few days later, he was off on another bender and verbally abusing her at home. The upshot was missed training sessions and an inevitable departure from another club that had tried to help him. 'It was such a shame, because everyone always showed willing to keep on giving George a chance, but there were limits and His Lordship always managed to reach them . . . he was, in so many ways, like a little pouting boy who would get upset when things didn't go his way but, unlike a child, who would tend to sulk when upset, George would just reach for the nearest bottle.'

On 3 May, a spineless display by Hibs handed Aberdeen the title at a windswept Easter Road. The Dons won the flag in style, pulverising Hibs 5–0. Steve Archibald and Andy Watson – both of whom would become Hibees in the future – give Aberdeen a 2–0 lead at the break. In the second-half, Ian Scanlon struck a brace and Mark McGhee also scored. With news coming through that St Mirren had held Celtic 0–0 at Love Street, Aberdeen manager Alex Ferguson bounded onto the pitch to congratulate his boys. When they arrived back in the dressing room, they found that the Easter Road bosses had kindly donated champagne, which had been bought in the vain hope of winning the Scottish Cup final the previous May! A few days later, the season ended in total indignity as only 1,191 turned up at Easter Road for the last league game of the season. Alex O'Hara scored as Partick Thistle won 1–0 after a mix-up between Craig Paterson and goalkeeper Huggins. Hibs failed to score for the eleventh time in 17 games. Substitute Peter Docherty was the twenty-ninth player to be used by the club in a season where the right mix on the pitch eluded Hibs until the bitter end.

Chapter Twelve

First Division

Attuning to life in the old First Division was never going to be easy for Hibs. Tom Hart estimated that the drop cost the club more than £200,000. But to give the chairman his due, he dug deep into his savings and work began to put things right on, off and under the pitch almost immediately. A £100,000 bid for St Johnstone striker John Brogan was unsuccessful when the club was unable to agree personal terms with the player, but plans were unveiled to lay under-soil piping at a cost of £60,000. Hibs, therefore, become the first club north of the border to install under-soil heating. Less welcome was the news that the three-year sponsorship deal with Bukta was about to come to an end. The cold financial realities of life away from the big league also meant that only four turnstiles for the main terracing would be opened on match days: at one time closing the entire terracing was considered as an option.

At the end of June, Tom Hart opened the new supporters club at Easter Road and gave a stirring oration to the troops, vowing to return Hibs to the top-flight in one season. And as for the gamble in signing George Best, the chairman was unrepentant: 'George Best was good for Scottish football and if I did nothing else, I must have got him to bed early at least one night!' The man himself was still in the States and word soon emerged that he would be a dad by the end of the year. He was back on form on the pitch, too, picking up two man-of-the-match awards from US football writers in June and also managing to find the net a couple of times. Hibs meanwhile embarked on a successful short tour of the Highlands, followed by a 1–1 draw at home with Swansea City. Arthur Duncan scored, but the highlight of the day was an appearance by local hero Allan Wells, who had just won the 100m gold at the Moscow Olympics.

The new league season opened on 9 August, but a last-minute goal by Ian Ballantyne condemned Hibs to a 1–0 home defeat against Raith Rovers. Off the pitch, Tom Hart revealed that Hibs fans may not yet have seen the last of Best. 'George is a signed Hibs player on the same contract as everyone, so he would be on the same money. We could not afford to repeat the special wages he was receiving last season. Southampton has shown an interest . . . we will see what happens when the American season ends in a few weeks. He sent us a postcard to wish us luck and promised to come north for a chat when he returns.'

Hibs won their first competitive game away from home in 17 months on 16 August, as a large travelling support saw them triumph 2–0 over Stirling Albion.* Peter Cormack scored his first competitive goal for the club since his return with a flashing drive and Gordon Rae added the second. Four days later, the good form continued when they beat Hearts at Tynecastle in the delayed final of the 1979 East of Scotland Shield. Hibs won a penalty shoot-out 5–4, after a 2–2 draw with their old rivals. A 3–0 home win over Berwick, thanks to a double from MacLeod and one from Paterson, helped keep spirits high. Next up was the Bells League Cup and a 2–0 win (Rae, MacLeod) over Alloa Athletic at Recreation Park. But the return leg at Easter Road saw the team lapse into their bad old habits, eventually jeered off the park following a tepid 1–1 draw. The only bright spot came when promising youngster Hugh Hamill scored his first goal for the club. At the other end of the age spectrum, John Connolly, newly freed by Newcastle United, signed for Hibs. Rae and MacLeod scored in a 2–0 win over Clyde at Shawfield in the League Cup and four days later a Willie Jamieson goal was enough to see off Motherwell in the league at Easter Road, but only 4,390 watched the game.

---

* Coincidentally that was the first Hibs game I'd seen in over a year, having been exiled in Stornoway. Maybe if I hadn't left Edinburgh, Hibs wouldn't have ended up in the mess they were in . . . or maybe not.

George returned to Scotland on 9 September, arriving in Edinburgh during the afternoon and immediately boarding the team
bus for the journey to Dundee. Tom Hart had put George in touch
with Ormond, who was faced with some injury worries for the
potentially tricky trip to Dens Park. George showed what a decent
guy he was by responding to the chairman's call with the words:
'I'll be there – I owe you a turn.' Against Dundee, he fired in a
cross for Gordon Rae to score 12 minutes from time to give the
Hibs a lucky 2–1 win. Dundee had most of the game prior to this –
though George did show some of the magic that had made life
tolerable for Hibs fans the previous season. Ally MacLeod scored
the opener before Jim Shirra brought the home side level. Looking
bronzed, fit and slim after his time in the States, where he had
skippered San Jose from midfield, George soon made another
gentleman's agreement with Mr Hart. It was unlikely that he
would settle in Edinburgh again and this time around, the deal was
that he would fly up from London just for the games. Hart
promised to sell the star to any English club willing to pay the
asking price of £60,000. George was growing increasingly aware
that he was running out of time and needed to earn as much
money as possible out of the game.

Best's name was missing from the team sheet for the 3–1 win at
Ayr United on 13 September, Hibs triumphing in his absence with
goals from MacLeod, Rae and Jamieson. The win put the Hibees
top of the table, but George's non-appearance was enough to set
tongues wagging. In actual fact, though, he had a prior engagement
to appear on an Ulster TV show and went with the club's consent.
He was missing again for the woeful 2–2 draw with East Stirling-
shire at Easter Road, where the promising Oxgangs youngster
Willie Jamieson scored both goals. Hibs had a late penalty claim
turned down and then Callachan hit the underside of the bar, but
the 'Shire held on for a draw.

One week later, George turned in another fine show as Hibs drew
1–1 away to Hamilton Accies. No disrespect to the Accies, but at
times like these George must have pondered what went wrong with
his career. Put it this way, Douglas Park isn't exactly the Bernabeau

Stadium, but to his credit George put in a good shift and his clever distribution of the ball was much appreciated by the large travelling support. Journalist Mike Aitken likened Best's appearance in Hamilton to Lord Olivier performing at Skegness Rep. Another veteran, John Connolly, scored his first goal for the club – a superb solo effort – in a game that Hibs should have won. Connolly took a pass from George just inside the Hamilton half, glided past the home defence and hit a scorcher from distance into the top left corner. The other veteran in green and white that day, Peter Cormack, must have also suffered a strange sense of déjà vu – he'd played as a fresh-faced teenager the last time Hibs had visited Douglas Park, 14 years previously in 1966!

Despite an invitation to play in the star-studded Franz Beckenbauer testimonial at New York's Cosmos Stadium, George flew up to Edinburgh the following week for the League Cup return match against Clyde. After a quick training session, he produced a peerless display, although he did manage to get himself booked. Earlier in the game, Clyde defender Jim Dempsey got his marching orders for a foul on the Northern Irishman. Hibs dominated the match and two goals from Willie Jamieson secured them a 2–1 win (4–1 on aggregate). Later, Best told reporters that his mind was made up: he intended to return to the USA and raise a family with Angie. Intriguingly, he later revealed that he and Angie would have considered living in Scotland long-term and were just about to look for a permanent home here. But he said that Tom Hart, with his team stuck in the lower league, no longer had the finance to afford the big wages. So both men agreed to call it a day and George sets his sights on the States. Until he made the move, though, he agreed to fly up for Hibs games when required and to train at Southend.

* * *

Only diehard Hibs fans will remember the name Terry Wilson, but he was the Fife miner who took on the thankless task of replacing Best in the Hibs squad. A £35,000 signing from Arbroath, Wilson

George admires a young starlet. *Scotsman*

was a good player though, and he made an immediate impact by scoring in the 4–1 home win over Clydebank. Connolly, Rae and MacLeod also got on the goal sheet. George did his bit to help younger players like Wilson and Derick Rodier by going out of his way to turn up for extra training in the afternoons. According to Derick, this was an 'incredible thrill' for him and all the other kids at the club.

George cancelled a scheduled flight to California to play for Hibs away to Dunfermline on 4 October. A large travelling support of just less than 3,000 made the trip to Fife for what was thought would be Best's last game for Hibs. He enjoyed a great reception and in return produced a master class in long cross-field passing during the game. Hibs, who – without Best – had lost 2–0 away to Dumbarton in midweek, won this game with ease. Ally MacLeod helped himself to a double, with the second and decisive goal being laid on for him by Best. Four days later, California must have seemed a million miles away as George lined up for the League Cup quarter-final first-leg at Somerset Park. The game against Ayr United was played out in miserable conditions, with a swirling wind making good football difficult. George had met his teammates in Glasgow, but arrived minus his travel bag that contained his football boots. Playing in a pair borrowed from Peter Cormack, Best performed well and set up the team's second goal for Ally MacLeod. Terry Wilson had scored first for Hibs and the team earned a hard-fought 2–2 draw. Best's presence helped boost the attendance to almost 5,000, the Ayrshire club's highest crowd of the season thus far.

Afterwards, it was revealed that Hibs had agreed Best's sale for £30,000 to San Jose Earthquakes. The deal – set up by American agent Dennis Roach – included a promise that the US club would play a friendly at Easter Road the following October. Best had set up the move earlier in the year in a series of late-night calls from Edinburgh to California, where his old Manchester United colleague Bill Foulkes was coach of the Earthquakes. After a meeting in London between the two men, George signed on the dotted line and celebrated with an orange juice. Commenting on his time in

Edinburgh, George said: 'I have thoroughly enjoyed being with Hibs. Chairman Tom Hart has done a lot to help me and I'd like to think I've repaid his belief in my ability. But the climate in California is what we miss most and that's where we want to settle.' He might also have added that he was heartily sick of all the media attention in the UK. In California he enjoyed relative anonymity and could walk into a bar and have a quiet drink without being hassled.

The *Evening News* on 10 October ran a story with the headline: 'Best of luck George – we'll all miss you.' The newspaper reckoned that every league club would be counting the cost of his departure because he had been 'Mr Box Office' during the previous year. Best, meanwhile, spent the early part of the week in Manchester saying goodbye to Sir Matt Busby and other friends at Old Trafford.

On 11 October 1980, George was made captain on his last appearance for the club. Connolly and Jamieson scored the goals in a 2–0 home win over Falkirk, but really the game was all about Best. Winning the toss, he decided to play up the slope and during the game he set up numerous chances for his teammates and came close to scoring on three occasions. One superb shimmy and left-foot drive that flew past the post drew gasps of admiration from the crowd. His final effort was a peach of a free kick that just hit the side netting. It would have been sweet to sign off in style, but George was still a happy man, he even shrugged off a story in the *Sunday Mail* the next day. The paper revealed that the Inland Revenue were pursuing the star for £17,000 and were preparing to file a bankruptcy notice. George responded: 'It's the first I've heard of this . . . I leave this kind of thing to my accountant.' And with that he disappeared into the sunset and headed off to a new life in California. Tom Hart meantime was taken into hospital for non-surgical treatment on a duodenal ulcer. Scurrilous rumours started to circulate around the city that the chairman and hospital staff had christened the ulcer George!

On 23 October Hibs, minus George, were knocked out of the League Cup, losing 4–2 to Ayr United on aggregate on a vile night, with rain sweeping down on Leith, watched by only 5,130. Afterwards, Tom Hart commented: 'George's association with Hibs has lasted just 36 days short of a year in which fans throughout Scotland have had the chance to watch a genius at work.' For his part, George said his time in Edinburgh had brought him closer to Angie and also shown him that there was hope in his battle with alcoholism. As he put it, 'the promises might prove empty, but the hope remains eternal'.

CHAPTER THIRTEEN

POSTSCRIPT

George once said that the football pitch was the place where he could escape from all the other hassles and demons that were assailing him. No matter what he might have said in his dark moods, he really did feel pleasure from playing well in front of large crowds and from being the centre of attention. Hopefully he enjoyed some of the games he played in Scotland, because he certainly brought a lot of happiness to those who watched him play. Cynics might point to the fact that George once likened his time at Easter Road to his spells at places like Dunstable and Stockport, where he was expected to do just enough training as required, show up for the games and do some tricks and bring in the crowds and the cash. His superior abilities meant that even operating in third gear, these games were 'easy money'. So the financial reward was undoubtedly one of the reasons for George coming north of the border. But he also once told the *Daily Express* writer David Miller that his time at Hibs was definitely not a gimmick and was much more crucial to him than his spell with Fulham.

Like many alcoholics, George often thought that a change of town or country would at least ease, if not solve, all of his problems. Rather than tackling the real causes of his alcoholism, he was running away from them. So in a way Edinburgh just joined South Africa, Marbella, Majorca, Dunstable, Cork, Los Angeles and Stockport as another stopping-off point on the denial road. In Edinburgh, though, he had a real opportunity to get his career back on track and also to put himself forward for a place in the 1982 World Cup. Tom Hart in particular offered the struggling star, who was still only aged 33, one final lifeline to save his career. In the end, he blew the chance but he gave a lot of people – not just Hibs fans – great memories during that year.

With the benefit of hindsight earned over the last 30 years, one can see that Tom Hart's good intentions, his attempt to act as a father figure to George, were ultimately misconceived. Indeed, the man himself was dismissive of the idea that Hart – or indeed Sir Matt Busby – acted as a father figure. Writing in his biography, *Blessed*, George said: 'The only sense in which you could describe him [Sir Matt] as a father figure was that, like my dad, he didn't really hand out any discipline . . . it might have been better for me if Matt had been harder on me. I had been getting away with things since I was a kid . . . as I got away with more and more it encouraged me to believe that I could do anything I wanted.' George – who had a lot of affection for Tom Hart – said that the Hibs chief's weakness in allowing him to return after suspending and sacking him was identical to Sir Matt's misguided lenience. It gave George the impression that it was OK to carry on binge drinking, to carry on missing training sessions and piling on weight, and to carry on letting people down. But Angie Best only has fond memories of the chairman who tried to help her errant husband.

'Tom Hart was a wonderful, colourful character and we both loved being in Edinburgh. They found us a lovely apartment and in many ways it would have been good to stay in Scotland long-term. But really, the fact that George showed up at all for Hibs was amazing and pure luck really.' Would things have been different if Tom Hart had taken a harder line? Probably not . . . as Angie herself sadly admits, nothing really worked for George.

As for Hibs? In the end, of course, George didn't save them from the drop, but as one wag put it back in 1979: 'A forward line of Batman, King Kong, The Bionic Man, Dan Dare and Charlie's Angels wouldn't be enough to save Hibs.' Even Tom Hart's belief that Best would boost attendances was ill-conceived. Despite the initial buzz of activity and the clank of turnstiles, interest soon tailed off. Indeed, even with the Best-inspired surge in attendances the average crowd for the 1979–80 season was only around 9,500.

* * *

His eventual departure from Easter Road didn't mean the end of his association with the club or, indeed, Scotland. One year on from leaving Edinburgh, George returned to fulfil a clause in the contract that had seen him leave for the States. San Jose Earthquakes, coached by the ex-Dundee player Jimmy Gabriel, played a challenge match at Easter Road on Monday, 5 October 1981, with the home side coming out on top 3–1. San Jose were the first NASL team to play at Easter Road and the match was a reciprocal game for the one Hibs played in California at the end of the previous season. (Hibs won 4–2 in San Jose on a tour that also saw them play Fresno and a Haiti select side.)

At the time of the Easter Road game, George was once again being touted for a place in Northern Ireland's squad for the 1982 World Cup in Spain. The national manager Billy Bingham was under pressure from the media to include the wayward star and attended the game. He left unimpressed, saying Best had lost his enthusiasm. Best also donned the Motherwell strip for 45 minutes when the Earthquakes played a friendly at Fir Park on the same tour. Also in 1982, with the taxman again banging on his door, George had to raise money quickly and did it in a succession of guest appearances. Accompanied by his latest flame, Miss World 1977, Mary Stavin, George turned out for both Arbroath Vics and Scone Thistle. George's friendship with Jackie McNamara ensured that he played one last time at Easter Road in August 1984, for Jackie's testimonial game against Newcastle United. Sadly, though, his old mentor Tom Hart wasn't there to welcome him back. Tom passed away suddenly in March 1982 after suffering a brain haemorrhage prior to a Hibs game at Pittodrie. He was treated at the stadium and then taken to Aberdeen Royal Infirmary, where he died shortly afterwards.

* * *

Without George, Hibs managed quite easily to climb back into the top division and there they have stayed, apart from one minor blip in the 1997–98 season. It would be wonderful to say that the football at Easter Road has been brilliant during the past 30 years, but two League Cup wins in 1993 and 2004 have been the only major successes. There was a while when, sitting in the back of the old East Stand every week, the only thing to look forward to were the guys who used to fire up joint after joint allowing all those sitting in the immediate vicinity to get nicely sedated during the games. Then came the smoking ban and even that option became a distant memory. Thankfully, though, Hibs fans could always rely on the special talents of players like Kevin McAllister, Keith Wright, Franck Sauzee and Russell Latapy to cheer us up on a cold day in Leith.

After leaving Scotland, George's career tailed away and by the mid-1980s he was finished with football. Unfortunately, without the game to focus on, the other great force in his life, alcohol, took over and his later years were punctuated by mishaps played out in the public eye. A string of failed relationships, a spell in prison in 1984, a disastrous drunken appearance on the *Wogan* show six years later and a liver transplant in 2002 are the episodes that stick in the mind. In the end, the power of his addiction overwhelmed his resistance and he passed away on 25 November 2005.

His funeral drew thousands of fans to the city of his birth, Belfast, and they paid their tributes as the funeral cortege passed from the family home to Stormont. Football clubs throughout Britain paid homage to the great man with a minute's silence observed at most grounds. At Easter Road, the players of Hibs and Rangers linked arms and bowed their heads as the silence began. But from the rear of the East Stand a ripple of applause began which slowly spread through the stadium. Those of an older vintage wiped away tears as memories drifted back through the years to the days when the world's greatest ever footballer played for their club – the days when George Best was a Hibee.

The tribute to George at Easter Road. *Press Association*

George's death led to a massive outpouring of emotion and support from his fans towards his family. Inspired by the amazing response, George's sister Barbara and her husband Norman set up the George Best Foundation in April 2006. The Foundation has a number of aims, including the promotion of a healthy lifestyle among children through football and sport-based initiatives, and to advise them on the dangers of drug and alcohol misuse. The Foundation also aims to provide funds to help medical research into illnesses associated with alcohol misuse. More details on how to donate to this very worthy cause can be found on the Foundation website at www.georgebest.com.

Chapter Fourteen

Memories of George

Alan Hart was the commercial director at Easter Road when George arrived in Edinburgh. The son of club chairman Tom Hart, Alan ran the lucrative Goldliner lottery that brought in vital cash for the team. Following his father's death in March 1982 from a brain haemorrhage and the subsequent takeover of the club by Kenny Waugh, Alan quit his post to set up his own property development company, though he remained on the Hibs board until the club was sold in 1987.

'My dad didn't like any derogatory things being said about Hibs, so he took it as a personal insult when the journalist Ian Archer wrote an article saying the idea of George joining Hibs was a joke. His immediate reaction was "right, I'm going to prove this guy is wrong and I'm going to get George Best to sign for Hibs."

'George came up to take in the Kilmarnock game as a guest and my dad took him and Angie for lunch at the Queensway Hotel. We used to call the Queensway "dad's office" because he used to spend so much time there. It had a lounge and very good restaurant and it was where all the directors had their meetings on Fridays. The first impression I had of George was that even though he was obviously a star, he was not a flash person. He came across as a very genial, quietly spoken fellow. In fact, Angie looked more like a superstar than he did.

'George's problem was that he was just too nice a person. After the games, the hangers-on would move in and offer to take him out drinking and George being George just didn't like to say no. He would help out with presentations and functions and would attend supporters' associations meetings where he would always take time to sign autographs. I remember George did things like open up the Kwik-Fit branch at Piershill, but at other events he would sometimes be left standing around at the end with no idea whether he was going to be paid or not. Around that time, Bill McMurdo, whom my dad had initially wanted to be commercial manager at Easter Road, became friendly with George and he helped to ensure that George was paid properly for these promotional events.

'My dad had a great affection for George, even though he often ended up tearing his hair out because of George's antics. The idea of getting him there was to lift the whole squad and it had the right effect on the crowds, it certainly got folks interested. But he didn't have the legs to make a difference on the football pitch. He would do one or two touches in a game that were brilliant, but it was never enough to get us out of the hole we were in. Whether that was because of the standard of the players he was playing with, I don't know. I suppose we all felt frustrated at the way things turned out, my dad would always try to give him another chance, and he didn't want the whole deal to end in failure. And George would always sound genuinely apologetic and say, "I'm sorry Mr Hart it won't happen again." That's just the way he was – George had his demons, but I don't think anyone who met him during his time in Edinburgh could fail to like him.'

Glasgow-born Alisdair 'Ally' MacLeod had spells with St Mirren (famously scoring four goals for The Buddies in one game against Rangers) and Southampton before signing for Hibs in 1974. He was perhaps the most skilful player at Easter Road before Best's arrival and a fine striker, scoring 71 times in 208 appearances for Hibs. He now works as an Independent Financial Adviser in Kirkintilloch.

'When he was at his peak, George was one of the best players I have ever seen. But when he came to Hibs we were having a hard time fighting relegation and sometimes he just wasn't what we required.

That's not taking anything away from the player that he once was. He used to just fly up on a Friday and take part in the training session, but even then Friday training was a time when we didn't really do much. He was quite out of shape, although the touch, the vision and the skill were all there. You could see what he was trying to do, but he just couldn't achieve it at times. His passing was still good, though, he was one of very few players I have ever seen who was so good with either foot that you couldn't honestly say which was his strongest.

Ally Macleod. *Copyright unknown*

'It was quite exciting when we heard he was coming, although the more experienced players knew that he was well past his best. Still, the aura of someone like George coming to play for Hibs was huge. It wouldn't be fair to say that there was resentment towards him or towards Hibs for bringing him, but you have to remember that he was getting paid a hell of a lot more than everyone else. He was getting two-and-a-half grand a game and sometimes we would be playing two games a week, which made it worse. But if there was animosity it certainly wasn't against George as a person.

'He was a smashing bloke, a lovely lad: great company and very down to earth, he ended up being just one of the lads. We would have a beer with him in pubs like the Jinglin' Geordie after training and he would tell us about his time with Manchester United and his birds – I think he spoke more about his birds than anything else. His wife Angie was a nice person too, very down to earth. I remember her asking me why a lot of the wives didn't go to the games.

'I would never say anything bad against George as a person; he was such a nice bloke. He was no mug either, but a bright intelligent guy, which makes you wonder about how he ended up, but obviously he had a disease. As a person, everyone got on with George, probably for the people in authority he could be infuriating but he was such a likeable chap that that would get him through no matter what.'

Arthur Montford worked for STV between 1957 and 1989 presenting Scotsport *and providing memorable commentary on many of the highs and lows of Scottish football. He has seen all of the great players of the modern era and has no hesitation in placing George as one of his top ten greats, alongside Scottish superstars like Law, Baxter and Johnstone. His favourite player, though, 'without a shadow of a doubt' was the English maestro Stanley Matthews; Arthur remembers Matthews playing alongside Billy Steel for Greenock Morton during the Second World War. Arthur met George during his spell at Hibs and the down-to-earth Northern Irishman left a favourable impression.*

'We invited George through to Glasgow one Sunday to appear on *Scotsport*. I asked him if I could organise a limousine for him and his then wife Angie, who was a lovely woman, to take them through from Edinburgh. He said, "no thank you, we will come through by train," which they did, and I told them to take a taxi from Queen

Street to the studio. George said, "not at all, we will just walk." We did a ten-minute live interview with him and he was on good form that day. I found him to be totally charming – he was very interested in how television worked from the studio point of view. I took him into the control room and introduced him to our director, Chris Allan, before the programme started and then he sat quietly in the green room waiting to go on.

'George did his interview with me, when he talked about his life and times, all the ups and downs along the way. He spoke very highly of his teammates at Easter Road – he thought they were a great bunch of lads. I offered to run him down to the station and he said, "no, no, what do you do after the show?" I told him that we usually have a cup of tea and he and Angie sat with us after the show, chatting away about the state of football. Two or three of the stage hands wanted his autograph and to take some pictures, which he agreed to do. He could not have been more helpful and more charming.

'When he was later in America playing for San Jose Earthquakes, I happened by coincidence to be in Los Angeles for a week doing interviews for a Radio Clyde programme called *Meeting Place*, in which I spoke to a number of people in the Hollywood area including Jack Lemmon, Charlton Heston and Johnny Mathis. So I went to the LA Coliseum to see Los Angeles play San Jose, who also had the ex-Dundee player Jim Gabriel in their side. After the game, I got to speak to George and he very kindly remembered his visit to the old *Scotsport* studio and he chatted away and asked me why I was in America. When I told him I was going to meet Charlton Heston the next day, George said, "oh be sure and ask him about the chariot race in *Ben Hur*," which I did of course. And that was the last time I ever saw George.'

Comedian, singer and actor Bill Barclay was born in South Lorne Place and went to school at Norton Park in the shadow of the Hibs ground. His career has seen him work with many of the greats of the entertainment industry, including Rod Stewart, Elton John and

Martin Scorsese – he played a part in the 2002 epic Gangs of New York. *When he was a kid, Bill sold crisps and chocolate to fans at Easter Road and watched his heroes like Tommy Younger and Joe Baker from the main terracing. One of his prize possessions is a rare video of George playing his last game for Hibs. Bill, who used to be the DJ at Easter Road on match days, provides commentary on the video.*

'I first met George in 1974 when I toured with Rod Stewart. We were all in Manchester and ended up in George's club. I arrived late with Billy Gaff, who was Rod's manager. When we got into the club, the bar had closed and George was sitting at the far end. I went up to him and said, "look, we are with Rod's party, is it OK if we have a drink?" And he just said, "it looks like your party has had enough." I remember thinking to myself, "what an arse! I think he was a bit annoyed because he was all alone at the bar while Rod and his entourage were all whooping it up!"'

'George's arrival at Hibs had an incredible impact. I remember reading Stewart Brown's first story in the *Edinburgh Evening News* and all the Hearts supporters were having a laugh, saying it would never happen. And then suddenly he was there. I was doing the sound and public address at Easter Road at the time and I remember the great atmosphere for George's first home game against Partick Thistle, with their manager Bertie Auld coming out and throwing his *Tom Thumb* cigars into the crowd. I have never seen so many Hearts fans inside Easter Road apart from at a Hibs–Hearts game – they were taking their families to the game just to see George.

'I got to know him fairly well when he was up here. I used to drive him and his wife back to their hotel after the game. People said he was only here for the money, but I remember one time I had been approached by a guy who wanted George to open some discos – one in Glasgow and the other in Dumfries on a Friday night. Now George was due to fly up to Scotland on the Friday, so the week before when I was driving him and his wife to the hotel I said to him, "I will drive you through to Glasgow and all you have to do is sign a few plastic balls and throw them into the crowd, then we nip down to

Dumfries and do the same. I'll have you back in Edinburgh by the back of ten and you'll get paid four grand." And George just looked at me and said, "Nah, no thanks!" So although he might have needed money like we all do, it wasn't the main thing driving him.

'I would see him after the games when he went to the old Supporters Club, which at the time was in a building just across the road from the main entrance. George was great company, but you never really got a minute with him, people were coming over all the time and trying to speak to him, offering him drinks.

'My greatest memory of him in a Hibs strip would have to be him scoring the goal against Celtic. The saddest part of it all was when he didn't turn up, like the time when he got drunk with the French rugby team. I was doing the sound at the Ayr United game and the place was packed. Tom Hart wasn't very pleased and he told me to announce that – for whatever reason – George would not be appearing that day. I said to him, "You tell them – I'll get lynched!" But I ended up making the announcement anyway. On another night, he joined me in the commentary box; we were going to be relegated and a lot of the crowd had invaded the park. I went into the dressing room and said, "George, will you come out and say something to the fans because they are all on the pitch." He said, "No problem." George just came out and apologised to the fans because the team was going down – it was quite an emotional night.'

Brian Johnson runs the Almondvale Programmes shop just 300 metres from Easter Road stadium. Back in 1979, he was a pupil at George Watson's school in Edinburgh and hardly ever missed a Hibs match.

'I went to every game home and away for about five years, so I must have been to every match George played for Hibs. I went through to Paisley for his debut on the Capital Supporters Bus. That game was quite surreal, just because of the amount of people who turned up solely to see him. Normally, you would get about 4,000 at these games but that day there was 13,000 plus there.

'I actually got to meet George once, before the friendly game down at Leicester. The game was played on a Monday and me and my pal Stevie Archibald skipped off school and got down on the Liberton supporters bus. I remember the weather was horrible, with snow on the ground when we arrived in Leicester. We got to the ground early, bought a programme and were just wandering around when the team bus arrived. I always remember George coming off and asking us, "what on earth are you doing down here on a day like this?" And we told him we were big Hibs fans who would go anywhere to watch the team, so he just handed us two free tickets for the centre stand! Even then, on a horrible night against Leicester who were not a great side, they still got a good crowd just because he was playing.

'George still had all the ability in the world, he was wonderful to watch, but he just didn't have the pace. He was always up for the big fixtures and he definitely raised his game for the matches against the Old Firm. But funnily enough, one of the best games he played was in the season after that, when he came back and played up in Dundee. They just could not do anything with him; he was laying the ball on a plate to everyone. Playing at that level, it would not have mattered if he was 45, he was just so good. And as well as being a wonderful football player, he was also a fantastic inspiration to the players around him. They improved because of him and obviously the crowd were buzzing every time he got the ball. His presence lifted the whole squad and OK we did get relegated, but the team was down before he even arrived. It was a poor side, the worst Hibs team I can remember, but three or four of the squad certainly raised their game because of him, especially Ralph Callachan.'

Brian Scott was a football reporter for the Scottish Daily Mail *when George arrived in Edinburgh in 1979. More than 30 years on, Brian still writes a popular sports column for the paper.*

'The assumption was that George was well past his best – everybody was aware of his wayward lifestyle. But Tom Hart was a bit different from other chairmen back then; he was willing to spend money if that meant bigger crowds and improving Hibs. Hart could be very convivial company, but he was a bit of tyrant, too.

'I was at George's debut at Love Street and I distinctly recall some of the senior players in the Hibs side were disinclined to pass the ball to him. I remember making this assertion in my match report. It was as if their noses were out of joint at the notion of him earning over £2,000 a game and they didn't want to be upstaged by him. One or two of them gave me a rather sour, brusque response next time I met them. Obviously my suggestion that they didn't want to play ball with George had been logged by them and they were thinking, "how dare you?".

'I remember George playing in a cup tie at Berwick Rangers and he was the most eye-catching player on the pitch. You could tell he wasn't the player he once had been, but his movement, his skills and the insight he had on the game had not left him. I spoke to him a couple of times at press conferences and he struck me as a guy who had no side to him. He didn't have any of the big-time affectations that some of the star players have nowadays. He was very warm and open, with a real charm. He came across as a nice guy.

'I recall once after a midweek game at Easter Road, I was with Gordon Simpson, who used to work for PA. We were preparing to head back to Glasgow and we decided to call in at this pub in the Haymarket. George just appeared with Bill McMurdo, who I think was his agent back then, and they sat a couple of places away from us at the bar. We exchanged a few pleasantries with them, George was very chatty and good company, but as we know he was never happier than when he was in good company at a bar. Tony Higgins tells a famous story about how he once got a telephone call from George on a Friday night, asking if he fancied going out for a drink. Tony lived in Glasgow and said something along the lines of, "Well George, I'd love to but we are playing tomorrow." Anyway, Tony really felt quite honoured that George had called him, so when he went through to the game the next morning he mentioned it to various mates and they all responded, "Oh, he phoned you as well!"

'As a postscript, the last time I encountered Best was maybe eight years ago, when he was signing copies of one of his books at the

Borders store in Glasgow. I went down to see him without any appointment and he was very busy with a long queue of people waiting. I managed to have a quick word with him and he was as friendly and charming as ever, but he looked ghastly and yellow-skinned. It was very sad to see him that way.'

Charlie Reid and his identical twin brother Craig have been lifelong Hibs fans. As The Proclaimers, they have become one of Scotland's most successful musical groups and their classic song 'Sunshine on Leith' is now Hibs' unofficial club anthem. They played a pivotal role in the Hands Off Hibs campaign in 1990 that thwarted Wallace Mercer's plan to merge the club with Hearts.

'When George signed, we were still living in Auchtermuchty and we used to travel down most weekends to see Hibs when they were at home. Where we lived in that part of Fife, there weren't too many Hibs fans, so we weren't in any supporters club. We used to get the bus or train down on a Saturday morning; and we would also travel to see them if they were playing at Tannadice or Dens Park. We used to stand on the main East terracing at Easter Road. Back in those days, they had just started to reduce the height of that terracing; I always thought that was a bad move.

'The first time we saw George play would have been his home debut against Partick Thistle. I always remember that because of the size of the crowd, we couldn't get our usual stance so we had to walk around to the cowshed end [Albion Place] of the terracing. I had been to a few games against Partick in the preceding seasons and they tended to be drawn-out affairs, either 0–0 or 1–1. Hibs were not doing so well then and would probably only get six or seven thousand of a crowd for a game against Thistle. But for George's debut there was a crowd of more than 20,000. I remember being amazed at the transformation that one player could bring. I also recall being at the back of the main stand when he walked around with his blonde wife, Angie; it was like seeing movie stars in Leith! She had on these long black boots and we were just standing there open-mouthed.

'Hibs were heading towards relegation that season and I suppose Tom Hart just decided to take a gamble. George brought many things to Hibs, like his experience and the bigger crowds, but I remember being at a game once – maybe it was up at Tannadice – when George didn't play and then you began to hear all these stories that he was an alcoholic and how sad that was. I'm guessing that we saw him play six or seven times for the Hibs. I remember seeing him on TV when we lived in England for a couple of years and how it all kind of unravelled for him at Manchester United. I suppose later on you get it all in perspective, put two and two together and realise that alcohol was his problem all along. You always wonder what would have happened if he had really worked hard at his game like, say, Dave Mackay did. God bless Hibs, I love them, but George should have been playing at a higher level back in 1979 and for years to come after that.

'And what does the whole episode tell me about Hibs? Well it proves to me that Hibs have always been a maverick club – that's what I love about them, they have been like that since the day they were founded. They have a wild streak to them and I hope they never lose it. Some of the decisions they made have not been great, but they are never a boring club. I am proud to say to my sons that I saw George Best play in a Hibs strip and that is a very happy memory that I will take to my grave with me.'

David Scrimgeour started working for The Scotsman *as a young lad in 1947 before moving to* The Daily Telegraph *12 years later. He became the* Telegraph's *Scottish correspondent before moving into the pub trade in the mid-1970s. He ran the Jinglin' Geordie when it was one of the busiest wee bars in Edinburgh – helping to slake the thirst of journalists from the nearby Scotsman building. Back in 1979, George Best was one of the pub's regulars, and David has nothing but good memories of the genial Northern Irishman.*

'Every Tuesday afternoon, the Hibs players would come in en masse after training. The pub was close to Waverley Station and the players came in for a drink before taking a train back to Fife or Glasgow. One day, who appeared with them but George Best, and he sat over at the fireplace with the rest of the players, cracking jokes; they were a great crowd of boys. The rest of the players would only stay for a couple of hours before going for their trains, and George was left behind. So I would often sit and chat with him. He was a most articulate wee fellow and very clean-spoken, especially compared to some of the modern-day footballers. I don't think I ever heard George curse or swear once in all the time I was in his company. And he was never boastful – there was nothing sleazy about him. He would talk a lot about his boyhood in Northern Ireland and what a wonderful place it was to grow up in. He was a very proud Northern Irishman. George wasn't keen on standing at the bar; he used to just sit quietly over by the open fireplace. There was never any trouble when George was around. He was always quiet and reserved and would just sit with his friends.

'One day, one of the paparazzi arrived and took a sly picture of George looking very forlorn and with a lot of glasses in front of him as the waitress had not cleaned the table. What that photographer did was most unkind. When he left the Jinglin' Geordie, he used to head back to the bar in the NB Hotel where he was staying. He used to find solace in drinking. George was so kind to the rest of the clientele in the pub: he would sign autographs or footballs for them, but mainly the regulars had enough sense to just leave him alone.'

Derick Rodier was a chemistry student at Edinburgh University when Eddie Turnbull signed him for Hibs at the start of the 1979 season. After leaving Easter Road, he played for Dunfermline and Berwick Rangers before becoming General Manager at the East of Scotland Premier League club Spartans.

'George was extremely friendly to everybody in the changing room and made no differentiation between senior and junior players in the way he spoke to people. He was quiet to begin with, but once he got to know people better, in particular the senior guys, he fitted in like any other person: laughing, joking, pretty much at ease. Young guys like me felt comfortable in his company and he did spend quite a bit of time in the younger players' company. In those days, you trained in the morning and then were free in the afternoon. The young guys would stay back to do some extra stuff or have a wee game in the gym. Best often played in these three-a-side gym games, long after the more senior guys had left. That was an incredible thrill for us all.

'One time, the coach John Lambie asked me and a player called Terry Wilson back in the afternoon by ourselves, to do crossing and shooting at one of the goalkeepers. George came out the tunnel and asked to join in. He proceeded to lash the first cross past the goalkeeper. Being a gambling man, John Lambie said he'd bet him he wouldn't do that again – but he did with the very next cross. For a guy of his size, I've still never seen anyone hit the ball as hard and as accurately as he could.

'I had never been in "superstar" company before and I was taken by the way he handled himself. He was friendly, modest and just oozed charisma. I only socialised once with him, but that day provided a perfect example of this charm. We had our Christmas day out in the Persevere Bar at the bottom of Easter Road. The senior guys always treated the younger guys to a lunch and a few drinks at that time of year. Best was late, due to giving an interview at the ground, but he came down once he'd finished. He could have gone off with better things to do, but he seemed to want to be part of it. The place was mobbed, so we squeezed him into a corner trying to keep him out the gaze. But within ten minutes, the word was out and there was a queue of people waiting to get his autograph. One lady asked him to sign a piece of paper seven times! He was patient and friendly with all of them. It was pure class. He left an hour or so later by himself, which surprised me.

'I remember that he dressed very well and generally looked immaculate. He was always perfectly groomed, his hair looked impossibly healthy. The senior guys used to give him stick for his toilet bag, which was actually more like a vanity case and contained shampoos and creams, most of which we'd never heard of. Back then, none of us really bothered and used whatever old bits of soap were lying around. Not Best. It's a norm for footballers these days, but it was unheard-of back then. It seems he was well ahead of his times again.'

Fred MacLeod was tour manager for Stewart's Melville FP Rugby Club's trip to Canada in May 1980. As part of the fundraising effort for the tour, a quiz night was held at the school. Fred, who would later become president of the SRU, invited his neighbour, Hibs star Ralph Callachan, and George to appear alongside other prominent local sportsmen on the panel. Also taking turns to answer questions were Scots rugby legends Douglas Morgan, John Rutherford and David Bell, hockey cap Chris Sutherland, basketball internationalist Jimmy Carmichael and Scotland's most capped cricketer, Ronnie Chisholm.

'It was a time when, fortunately, George was off the drink and he readily agreed to participate. Some 200 pupils and 100 parents attended the evening, and there was great excitement at the thought of George taking part. As it turned out, he was the star of the show and, not only did he answer most questions on football, but he excelled in the field of horse racing, getting every question right. The audience could not fail to be impressed and George's answers were met with rapturous applause by his wife at that time, Angie, who shouted and clapped from the back of the hall.

'The quiz was a close affair and came down to virtually the last question on lacrosse, which, unfortunately, the quizmaster got wrong. Regardless, it was a memorable evening for all who attended and George's behaviour was impeccable. At the end of the quiz, he went down from the platform into the floor of the hall and patiently signed about 200 autographs and spent a good deal of time chatting to everyone. Afterwards, the panel was invited to the Principal's study, where the Principal was charmed by a somewhat noisy Angie.'

New Zealand-born Graeme Wright was the co-author of George's 1981 autobiography Where Do I Go From Here?, *one of the better books written about Best. During his research, Graeme lived with George, Angie and their Alsatian dog Dallas in their flat on Palmerston Place. Graeme, who lives in London, went on to edit the cricketer's bible,* Wisden.

'The book I did with George was published by Macdonald Queen Anne Press and I had been managing editor there some years earlier. The publishers feared that George might be difficult, given his reputation, and knew that I would be patient with him. They also knew I would be available at certain times when I was not working on *Wisden*, and when they asked me if I would be interested in working with George I agreed.

'Just before I met him for the first time, he had that weekend when he went on a bender with Jean-Pierre Rives and the rest of the French rugby team. After that, he and Angela left Edinburgh and came down to London for a while. I met them in their flat in Putney. That was them vetting me; they wanted to see if they liked me. There was a spare bedroom in Palmerston Place, so we agreed that I would go up and spend a week with him. In the end, I went up for three different periods of time. My family come from Aberdeenshire originally, so getting the chance to spend some time in Scotland was really nice for me. But also living with him was a good way to get to know George and see how he spent his days. As far as I recall, I don't think he drank again while he was at Hibs. He lived a very quiet life. He would train in the morning – George loved training and playing football. In the afternoons, we would sit down with a tape recorder and talk. In the evenings, we would mostly eat in and watch TV, though occasionally we would eat out in a restaurant. From his point of view, working on the book was great because it meant he had something to fill his time. In the past, he had sometimes suffered from that horrible footballer's syndrome of going to training and then afterwards there was not much else to do.

'He liked Edinburgh because the people treated him fairly normally. He was very much of the Scotch-Irish Protestant tradition and he felt at home in Edinburgh; in some ways more than he would living in Belfast, because in Edinburgh people just let him have a normal life. George loved talking, but the hard part was keeping him on subjects that I wanted him to talk about. It was also difficult sometimes working out what was real and what wasn't. I don't mean he was being untruthful. More that there was an element of him wanting to remember the past in a certain way. He saw things in his own mind differently sometimes to how they really were. After doing those tapes, I went to Manchester and spoke to people like Pat Crerand, Mike Summerbee and various non-footballer friends he had who maybe owned clubs or hairdressers. That allowed me to get their side of the story and see if it matched up to his. Sometimes it didn't. I don't think George was deliberately sending me down the wrong track; it was just the way he remembered things.

'He genuinely felt aggrieved that nothing went right at Manchester United after they won the European Cup. That became a fixation for him and he would come back to that time and again when we talked. He was grateful to Hibs for allowing him the chance to play. But he sometimes felt frustrated there, and I suspect he had had a similar problem latterly at Manchester United. Like any great player in many sports, George did not always appreciate just how much better he was than those around him. If he could see a pass, he couldn't understand why one of his teammates had not read it. It seemed so obvious to him that that was where the ball should be played. Denis Law or Bobby Charlton might have been there for it, but someone playing for Hibs or whoever maybe just didn't have that same vision. It's like watching a game on television. If you have the right camera angle, you sometimes see exactly where a ball should be played, and you wonder why the player on the ball doesn't make that pass. George had terrific vision of where the opposition were on a football field. What was also frustrating for him was that not only did no one run onto the ball, but the crowd would get on his back for giving the ball away. I watched him play a few times for Hibs and I could see what he meant, but he was asking too much of the other players. He didn't lack sympathy for them. It was just that he really didn't have the understanding that not everyone played the game his way.

'When we talked about his drinking, the term he always used was that he was a bout alcoholic. He believed that the problem was in his blood and provided he stayed off the booze, he would be all right. The trouble was that he couldn't stay off the drink. He didn't need to drink everyday; he wasn't that type of alcoholic. I wouldn't deny that he was an alcoholic, but the time I spent with him I began to wonder if the underlying problem was that he suffered from depression. F. Scott Fitzgerald was an alcoholic, but as I understand it he wasn't a bottle in the drawer every day type of alcoholic. He drank when everything was going great in his life. He needed to be at the bottom and climb back up again. That gave his life a purpose. I felt that George was the same way inclined.

'George was a great one for watching quiz programmes on television and he answered questions that I would never know the answers to. You could get into conversations with George about all types of things. In the book we did, there is a mention of a Peter Sellers film called *Being There*, based on a book by Jerzy Kosinski. Now, George read that book and it was him who told me about it. George was an intelligent guy, he just had one problem and that was, once he started drinking he couldn't stop.'

In 1980, Helge Åmotsbakken was a 30-year-old globe-trotting journalist for one of Norway's leading investigative magazines, Vi Menn. Helge later held senior posts in journalism, corporate communications and currently works for a large Nordic retailing company. Helge was the reporter who broke the story of George's drinking binge that led to his sacking from Hibs. Thirty years on, he still has vivid memories of his day spent in the company of the world's most famous footballer.

'After having worked for weeks through various channels and contacts, I managed to broker the interview with George, at a cost of £5,000. On the day, the interview as such never occurred, but I still ended up getting some good quotes from him. First of all, we got a lot of good pictures taken at the ground, but then George wanted to take us to a pub. Until that specific moment, he had been a real treat, very polite and close to being humble. He was enjoying a laugh with us and he was very far from the image of the world's most famous footballer.

'I was well aware of his problems with alcohol and his one-way contract with Hibs, so I asked him, "Are you sure it is a good idea to go to the pub? Shouldn't we go to a restaurant and treat you to a nice, quiet meal instead?"

He looked at me straight and replied, "Look, you are not my minder and I can handle myself. It is your choice. I want to go to the pub and you are free to follow."

'We arrived at the pub just after noon and spent five hours there with George and a few teammates. Early on, George had a couple of Cokes and he chatted to me about his regrets and how alcohol had disrupted his career. "Booze and birds, you know, is not an ideal combination for an athlete. I should have known better, but I have had too many 'friends'," he said. Then he asked me very politely to get him a beer. I again expressed my concern, in a polite manner. He then turned somewhat aggressive and ordered one of his teammates to get him one. From then on, it went downhill.

'When we left the pub around 1800 hours, his voice was slurred. We had spoken a bit during this drinking session, with some quotes I decided not to print. When leaving, he offered to return the cheque of £5,000, asking if I was "disappointed." I refused and thanked him for having allowed us to spend so much time with him.

'My editor in Norway was very happy, though, especially when the story of his sacking broke and we sold a record number of copies with our exclusive story!

'In retrospect, I felt very sorry and sad for this genius of a footballer, especially having met with his two-sided character: the modest, almost shy Belfast boy, and the more aggressive victim of fame.

Iain Gray, MSP for East Lothian, is the leader of the Labour Party at the Scottish Parliament. He has been following the Hibs for almost 50 years and has seen many great performances – Pat Stanton's outstanding display against Juventus is a particular favourite – and he also has some funny memories of his times at Easter Road. (Iain remembers Arthur Duncan eating a custard cream biscuit during a game that had been handed to him by a fan in the old enclosure!) But the best player Iain ever saw in a Hibs strip was undoubtedly George Best – he recalls that some of the things the Northern Irishman could do with a ball were almost supernatural.

'I first started going to Easter Road when I was five. My grand-father, George Cumming, used to work on the gates and one of his pals used to take me and we would watch the first-half together, then George would join us at half-time. (Back then, they used to shut the turnstiles at half-time.) The first game I saw was against Kilmarnock and we won 2–0. Back then, we would usually stand in the enclosure under the old main stand, but for that first game we sat in the stand. I can still remember walking up the steps, it was quite a sunny day and I was really impressed by the scale of the ground and the greenness of the grass. That first game, we sat on one of the old benches in the stand and I can still remember everyone leaping up when Hibs scored. I wasn't really sure what to do – but I caught on quick!

'By the late 1970s, I was married and living in Wester Hailes. My initial reaction on hearing that Best had signed was mixed. I'm no fan of celebrity signings, but Hibs were having such a dire season that I suppose George gave the fans something to latch onto. My first wife was heavily pregnant at the time – and I very seldom used to go to away games anyway – but when George made his debut at Love Street we drove through to see him. I remember the ground being packed, but in the first-half George did nothing and Hibs were pretty poor. We went 2–0 down, but soon after that, Best got the ball and my recollection is that it was almost like the St Mirren defence just disappeared in front of him and he walked through them and lashed it into the net. He was overweight and very slow, but he was still capable of these flashes of brilliance. Soon after-wards, he got the ball again and did exactly the same thing again and hit the post. So he very nearly took it back to 2–2 on his own.

'I wouldn't say that he treated the games with contempt, but near the end of games he would play closer and closer to the tunnel so that when the final whistle blew he didn't have that far to walk! When he ran towards an opposing player, he didn't even need to send them the wrong way to go past them – they would just fall over and he then walked past them. The other thing which was quite bizarre was that when he played a pass, it was almost as if he still had control over the ball when it had left his foot! The ball would just land at the feet of the player it was meant for in a way that was just so perfect. When he played a pass, you could almost taste the quality. I've seen a lot of great players – growing up my favourite players were the characters in the team, people like Arthur Duncan, Eric Black, Eric Schaedler, and Pat Stanton, of course. But I have never seen a player who could do some of the things that George Best did. In terms of his overall contribution to the club, he obviously wasn't the greatest ever Hibs player. But, of all those I've seen in a Hibs strip, George Best had the greatest ability.'

Ian Wood worked initially as the art editor's assistant on The Scotsman, *then did a stint as copytaker. He subsequently worked on the sports, news, and foreign desks before rising through the ranks to become sports editor. Over the years, he has covered many big football games at home and in Europe and seen many of the great players in action. Billy Steel of Dundee and Tommy Pearson of Aberdeen were two of his favourite players to watch. For Hibs, Ian has fond memories of the Famous Five (Gordon Smith was a particular favourite) and of Alex Cropley, Peter Marinello and Alan Gordon. After working at North Bridge for 40 years, Ian took early retirement in 1994, though he still writes a popular column for the newspaper.*

'When George arrived, Hibs were already in a bit of trouble and heading for the lower division. His coming delayed things, but of course he didn't manage to save them. Like everybody else, when I first heard the rumour he was signing my reaction was along the lines of, "aye, that'll be right." Then when it happened, I had to join in the dash of reporters to the airport for his arrival, but in typical George fashion, he never came on the flight he was scheduled to be on! Tom Hart was the main motivating force behind the move and it was quite a bold gamble for him to take. But he wasn't the first – or the last – who thought that he could handle George and take him under his wing, act as a father figure, just like Matt Busby had tried to be. But George had proven many times before that that just didn't work with him.

'I managed to talk a lot to George during his time at the club. He was a charming wee man, he could have charmed the birds off the trees. George was always courteous, helpful and cheery, even though every Tom, Dick and Harry was pursuing him. But he never lost patience with these people, in fact he was more likely to ask them to join him for a drink, which was the worst thing they could do because they would never get home! I used to be in his company in the Fleshmarket Steps pubs, the Jinglin' Geordie and the Half-Way House. I wouldn't say I was one of his cronies, just about everybody who was on the scene back then had a drink with George at some time or another. The regulars in these pubs just latched onto him and he became one of them. He wasn't there that long, but he was quick to find the best places. Hibs had him in the NB Hotel on the weekend of the big rugby game – that was a big tactical error. That was like waving a red rag to a bull! He shouldn't have been anywhere near that hotel that weekend.

'George always seemed to find room on the pitch and he never appeared hurried, even though he was the most closely marked footballer in Scotland at the time. I remember someone stabbed a hard diagonal pass towards him during a game. It was a difficult pass to take, but he didn't even bother. He stepped over it with his right foot and the ball shot through and then he brought his left heel behind him and used it to angle the ball to one of his teammates, who was waiting for a pass out on the wing. This poor guy had obviously never seen a pass like this before and the ball just rolled past him and out of play. George just sort of looked at this guy with his hand outstretched as if to say, "Aw come on." It was so slick and controlled – the type of thing Maradona or Pele would do. George was overweight, but even so he was always going to prosper in that league. If he'd applied himself, he could have played on here for years. The opposition were all petrified that he was going to make a fool of them, so they held back and that gave him the time. He was a real artist on the ball.'

The Trainspotting *author Irvine Welsh grew up on the Muirhouse estate in Edinburgh, where he used to kick a ball around with another young fanatical Hibee, Middlesbrough manager Gordon Strachan. Irvine's boyhood idol was Pat Stanton and he remembers being lifted over the Easter Road turnstiles and running wild on the empty terraces with his mates long before kick-off on match days. By 1979, Irvine had moved to London and so missed out on seeing many of George's games for Hibs, but in his novel* Glue *the main characters attend a Hibs match that Best competes in. The crowd sings, 'His Name is Georgie Best'. Irvine, who now splits his time between Miami and Dublin, was one of thousands who paid tribute to George at the star's funeral.*

'I met George Best once at a *Loaded* magazine do, where he confessed that a combination of factors like drink, travel and relationship breakdowns meant that his time at Hibs was a bit of a blur. But he spoke highly of Tom Hart and he thought the boys at the club were a great bunch. He intimated to me that he found the goldfish bowl vibe of Edinburgh similar to that of Manchester, and was much more comfortable in blasé London, as you'd expect.

'I saw George play for Hibs a few times, most notably against Rangers at Easter Road when we won 2–1, and the depressing 5–0 cup semi-final defeat by Celtic at Hampden. I remember hitchhiking from London to see him against Morton at Easter Road, but he went AWOL, Willie Murray took his place and played a blinder in a 3–2 win.

'My mate Dougie Webster from Muirhouse also saw George play in some of those games. Dougie lives in Sligo and we decided that we'd go to George's funeral in Belfast for old time's sake. We went up just for the funeral. I ran into a journalist on the *Observer* I know and he kept asking me who I was doing a feature on it for, I don't think he believed me when I told him I was just up paying my respects as a fan.

'The funeral was an incredible event – Northern Ireland's first big non-sectarian occasion. People were waving Hibs banners and Manchester United flags. To my mind, that was the day the province came of age. It was like a great big party in the pissing rain – Catholics and Protestants, people from north and south of Ireland, all standing together, yet there was no bother.'

Jackie McNamara. *Copyright unknown*

Jackie McNamara came to Hibs in an unpopular swap deal that saw club legend Pat Stanton sign for Celtic. Jackie eventually won over the Easter Road support and in 1979 the Hibs Supporters

Association named him player of the year for the second season running; the first Hibs player to have won the honour twice in a row.

'To start with, there was disbelief among the players when we heard that George was coming to Hibs, but when it happened he turned out to be a decent human being, he was a nice lad. Socially, George fitted in well, but the problem was he was flying down south after games. Regarding his wages, we decided at the start of the season that if any of the players won any money, like for man-of-the-match awards in the cup games, we would put it into a kitty for a Christmas night out in the Persevere Bar in Leith. Some of the young boys got £50 for playing in a five-a-side tournament down in Peebles and didn't put the money into the kitty. That caused a bit of animosity and George took umbrage at that, he thought we were having a go at him, but we had to explain that it had nothing to do with him and we soon got that sorted out. We were on about £120 a week plus £30 a point bonus. And of course George was on £2,500 per game. I suppose that caused a bit of animosity, you see we had a team of journeymen and the manager wanted to keep us all on the same wages, unless you were a youngster coming through, when you were on £70 a week.

'We used to go for a pint or two to Leery's Lamplighter on Dublin Street and the first couple of times we went out with George, we were in the Terrace Inn on Montrose Terrace, which was called Sinclair's back then. But the Jinglin' Geordie was popular because it was so close to the railway station for us. Eddie Turnbull used to hammer us hard at training on a Tuesday and shout, "It's OK boys, you'll be in the Jinglin' in an hour!" He knew exactly what was going on and he didn't mind because it helped the guys to bond as a group. When George was out on the town, people would pester him; old grannies would go weak at the knees when they saw him! But George was a very humble guy and he found time for all these people and signed autographs for them. There was no Billy-Big-Time about him at all. He liked socialising and he was a social drinker, he just liked the company and a game of darts and a beer, just to relax. It must have been stressful for him, but he was a very gentle guy – I never saw any sign of aggression from him.

'I had never been dropped by Hibs, but it happened on the day we played Rangers at Ibrox – Tony Higgins was left out, too. George was in seeing the doctor to get a jag and wee Willie Ormond was in the dressing room and told us not to say anything, but that George was drunk. Eddie Turnbull then told us that George was getting treatment for a virus and Tony said, "But Willie, you told us George was drunk!" Peter Cormack was in the team, too, and he could hardly walk because of his swollen knee. Tony turned to me and said, "McNamara, we must be really good players when a cripple and a drunk can get a game before us." That was the only time playing with George that I was aware that he was drunk during a game . . . it was quite evident.

'He did me the honour of playing in my testimonial game against Newcastle United. I wanted to get my old club Celtic to play but that wasn't possible – to be honest you could put 11 Alsatians in Celtic strips and the fans would still turn up to see them. So we got Newcastle instead and tried to get Kenny Dalglish to guest, but he couldn't make it, but George agreed straight away. The referee that day was George Smith, a lovely guy but quite a strict referee, he pulled George up saying, "You come here." And George wouldn't go to him and he picked the ball up and shouted at the ref, "See all these people in the crowd, they came to see me, not you." Then he saw me out of the corner of his eye and added, "Oh aye, and they've come to see Jackie too!"

'We went over to Belfast after being asked by the local Hibs Supporters Association and we laid a wreath from all the former players at his graveside. I went with Lawrie Reilly, Billy Hunter, who also played from the great Motherwell team of the 1960s, Ralph Callachan and Willie McEwen, who is a big Hibs fan. Meeting George's sister was lovely. It was quite a grey day weatherwise and seeing all the tributes by the grave was quite emotional for us, I've lost a few good friends who I played football with and George was one of them. In the end, we are all specks of dust aren't we?'

Jimmy O'Rourke was one of the most popular and talented members of Turnbull's Tornadoes, forming a classic striking partnership with Alan Gordon. A lifelong Hibee, one of Jimmy's proudest moments was when he scored in the 1972 League Cup Final.

'I always found George to be a real gentleman. He was very charismatic, but he had time for everyone he met, from the tea lady to all his teammates. I didn't get to see him play much because I was reserve team coach back then and we would usually be playing away from Easter Road on the same day. But George just had a God-given talent to play football. Maybe it's true that he didn't have the speed that he used to have, but once a genius, always a genius.'

Lifelong Hibee John Hislop was only a boy when George scored the decisive goal in the European Cup final in 1968, but he knew enough about football to realise that he had witnessed a genius at work. John joined Lothian and Borders' finest in 1978 and after 30 years with the police, he is now training to be a journalist.

'I have always loved football; even to this day I remember Pele in 1970, Cruyff in 1974 and Maradona in 1986. In my view, there is only one name that could be added to that list, and I saw him play for Hibs. In fact, he nearly got me sacked.

'Even in the late 1970s, I never missed a home game. Although the football was poor, I felt that this was payback for the hours of excitement the Tornadoes team had given me. One ambition, though, was to see George Best play. There were rumours of a comeback, and I decided that wherever he played in Britain, I would go, just so I could tell my grandchildren that I had seen George play live.

'When the *Evening News* broke the story that he had signed for us, I could not believe it. At that time, I was Police Constable 232C working at the West End Police Station, and in the following days, I was too happy to arrest anyone. I can't remember ever being so excited about anything as George's home debut against Partick Thistle. I was due to be working on an early shift that finished at 1.45 p.m., so I would have plenty of time to make the kick-off. But a few days before the game, I learned that my shift had been changed to 10 a.m.–6 p.m. and I would be working at the game. I would have preferred to watch from the terracing, but at least I would see the action. There was always the possibility that I would be given the pitch detail and see him close up.

'On the day of the game, I turned up for the briefing at 1 p.m. As the numbers were read out, I heard the fateful words. "232 you are working in the car park." I am convinced to this day that the miserable old git of an Inspector knew the effect this would have on me. Although I had only met him a couple of times before, I suspected from his dour, humourless manner that he was a Hearts fan. In his defence, however, my reaction to a Hibs goal in a previous game when, forgetting I was in uniform, I hugged my colleague and shouted, "Yes," may have also clouded his judgement.

'At two minutes to three, I was alone in the car park at the back of the big terracing. There was a massive crowd and I could feel the tension rising. I had to make a decision. Running up the numerous stairs, with my raincoat flapping in the wind, I gave no thought to the potential consequences. I had to at least see George running out the tunnel, which I did. The game passed by in a blur, although I did nip back to the car park at half-time hoping that no cars had been broken into.

'My abiding memory of the game was a free-kick, which George took from some distance away. My mind may be playing tricks, but I think he hit the ball from Lochend Road before Alan Rough tipped it over the bar. Anyway, I do remember that we won 2–1. After the game, I was summoned to see the Inspector, whose face was the colour of a Hearts strip. Apparently, there had been a "Turnhouse emergency." A plane was having problems with its landing equipment and all available emergency services were summoned to the airport. When they checked the car park, there was no sign of me, and he demanded to know why.

'The one good thing about joining the police in the 1970s was the training given by older cops who drummed into me from the start that under no circumstances should I ever admit to doing anything wrong. "I spotted three guys trying car doors and took off after them," I lied. We both knew I was lying, and after two minutes of threats he gave up and stormed away, although he did phone my Superintendent about it. Many years later, I bumped into Eddie Turnbull in Stockbridge. We got talking about football and the glory days of the 1970s. At one point, I mentioned George Best. "Him?" the great man said, "he got me the sack." He nearly got me the sack as well, I thought.'

Manchester United fan Paul Collier, who helped George research two of his autobiographies, remembers seeing the Northern Irishman play for Hibs at Parkhead in March 1980. At the time, Paul was aged 19 and living in Bearsden, Glasgow and occasionally travelled to games with friends on a Milngavie Celtic supporters' bus.

'I knew this game was coming up against Hibs and I had been a fan of George for as long as I could remember. I was born in Manchester and my Dad had always been a huge United fan, so it was inevitable that I would support the club, too. Unfortunately, I didn't get to see George in a live environment until November 1971, when United played at Stoke City. Sadly by then, George was on the decline – most people say he was at his peak from 1963 to 1968. My Dad told me that when George was 17, he was unstoppable. Seemingly, opposing defences just didn't know what to do with him.

'It seemed quite surreal to see George play in a Scottish league game. I recall quite vividly thinking that he looked overweight and unfit. My other abiding memory of George that day was just how short his shorts were! They were too small and too tight! I was standing behind the goal at the Celtic end of the ground, but I remember the Celtic fans in The Jungle giving him some good-hearted stick – probably because he was a Protestant. He, in turn, gave them some stick back. But it all seemed very light-hearted and I am sure the Celtic fans were really quite happy to have the chance to watch George play. Obviously, his legs had gone, but I do remember him hitting two or three fantastic 40-yard passes and thinking, "Blimey, he may not be able to run very much any more, but he can still pass the ball!" On the day, Hibs were well and truly outplayed and the 4–0 scoreline reflected that. In truth, it would have taken a lot more than George Best in his prime to have kept Hibs up that season.'

Paul, who had idolised George from an early age, later got to meet his hero on a number of occasions after he approached the star's agent, Bill McMurdo, a few years after George had left Easter Road. Paul wanted to get some items of memorabilia signed and met George at a promotional evening at the Scottish Motor Show in Glasgow in 1985. He went on to become a good friend of the Northern Irishman.

'It got to the point where George and his best friend and later agent Phil Hughes used to phone me up when they needed to check some dates or details about George's life. I remember Phil phoned me once to find out when George's divorce from his first wife Angie had come through! In 2001, they asked me to check the manuscript of his book *Blessed* – in all honesty I would have paid them to do it! I did it in three days and must have corrected some 130 factual and statistical errors! I ended up doing the chronology and George's playing statistics for that book and the update and fact-checking again for the follow-up, *Scoring at Half-Time*.'

Paul, who went on to be an author in his own right, penning the excellent account of the 1971 Ibrox Disaster *Stairway 13*, has fond memories of the Northern Irishman and recalls a man who was the antithesis of the hedonistic star portrayed in the tabloids.

'George was a very quiet and unassuming man with a great sense of humour – he was genuinely very witty. The last thing he ever came across as was a superstar. He used to listen very intently to what people had to say to him, and then he would evaluate it and give you a measured answer. Incidentally, I never saw him drink a drop of alcohol in all the times I met him. In fact, his real passion was for a good cup of strong tea!'

Ralph Callachan was the Hibs supporter who started off playing for Hearts before ending up at Easter Road via a short spell at Newcastle United. A skilful midfielder, he was also capable of scoring spectacular goals – Stewart Brown of the Evening News *reckoned Ralph's solo effort against Dundee in August 1979 was one of the greatest goals he had ever seen. After giving up football, Ralph worked for almost 20 years in the pub trade with his friend and golfing partner Jackie McNamara.*

'My family are from the Lochend area and my dad was a big Hibs fan, so when I signed for Hearts in 1973 he maybe wasn't too sure about the whole thing! But I just wanted to play football and Hearts were good enough to offer me a chance. I really enjoyed my time at Tynecastle – they had a manager, John Haggart, who did a lot to improve my game. Around the time I joined Hearts, they had a lot of good young players, like Willie Gibson and Sandy Burrell, and the season I broke into the first-team I played in the 1976 Scottish Cup final against Rangers.

'It was hard to get to know George well, because he was only coming up on the weekends and often he would just head out to the airport after the game on Saturday and fly off to wherever he was going. When he did train at Easter Road, back then it was the normal thing for players to go out together and have a pint. George just seemed to feel really comfortable doing normal things like having a game of darts with the boys. But afterwards, everyone would go their own way and George would be stuck alone in the hotel on Princes Street. It wasn't a normal lifestyle; it must have been very difficult for him to deal with. George was one of the greats for sure, but also as a person he was a good lad. Of all the people who got to know him up here, very few would criticise him.

'George was just a down to earth guy, there were no airs and graces about him. He loved to talk about sport – and he would talk to anyone who approached him. I wouldn't say he was harassed, but if he walked outside it could be difficult for him to really enjoy the place. So you can understand the predicament he must have been in at times, he was such a good guy that he would get involved with most people. It wasn't hard to predict what might happen when he was staying in the hotel on the night before a game with the whole French rugby team! The way that worked out was disappointing for Hibs, who are a big club, and on that occasion he let us down. He let the players down and he let the likes of Mr Hart down. Mr Hart, the chairman, had taken a chance on him and although he did lift the club to a certain extent, when he looked back on that particular episode George would have been very embarrassed.

'As a player, obviously the pace was no longer there, but you could see that his football brain was still sharp. At times he could make people look stupid just by the dip of his shoulder. You have to remember that he was at the end of his career, sometimes he would try passes that weren't really on. It was best to play the ball to his feet, and then if he was around the 18-yard line he could maybe do something special with it. It was a pleasure to play with the guy and it would have been great to play with him in his heyday.'

Simon Pia was born to be a Hibee. His dad was a Hibs-daft Edinburgh Italian who worshipped Gordon Smith and Joe Baker and who took Simon's mum on a first date to a Hampden semi-final against Motherwell in 1947. Simon's first game was a heavy defeat against Hearts in 1962, but it's been uphill ever since. He has idolised players like Willie Hamilton, Big John McNamee, Pat Stanton and Jimmy O'Rourke. Simon, who has written a couple of great Hibs books, now works as a press officer for Scots Labour leader Iain Gray and he can be found with his four brothers and his son in the old North Stand every other Saturday.

'Back in 1979, I was a student in London. One Sunday morning I was on my way home passing through King's Cross when I spotted a headline in a newspaper rack – "Guess Who's Coming to Hibs?"

A bit hung-over, I snatched the paper – the *Sunday Mail* – from the rack and there was a picture of Bestie. That woke me up. Immediately, I ran across the concourse to the nearest phone and called my brother, David, who lived in Richmond. I got him out of his bed. "You won't believe it. George Best is coming to Hibs!" "What? You're having me on." "No, no. It's true. Honest. George Best is coming to the Cabbage. It says so in the *Sunday Mail.*"

'The next Saturday found both of us at a game at White Hart Lane. We rushed out at the end to David's car to catch BBC's *Sports Report* and any news from Love Street. Sure enough, the dulcet tones of Ian "Dan" Archer came crackling down from Scotland and we hung on his every word. Georgie was a Hibee. The fact that we lost didn't really matter. The *Sunday Mail* picture had gone up on my wall, but I had to wait till I was back home before I saw George in the flesh. It was against Rangers, three days before Christmas. That day, we were in the old enclosure and joined the adults pushing aside the wee boys who usually hogged the wall at the tunnel as we leaned over to catch sight of Bestie.

'Smaller than I expected, he trailed up out the tunnel last man onto the pitch, rubbing his hands, shoulders hunched. He looked as if he had a hangover and hadn't shaved for a week. He had a wee pot belly and a bit of a double chin. Still, I was transfixed. A guy on my shoulder said, "Look at the bulge in his breeks." Such was the effect of his reputation on some people. It was a frosty, bone-hard pitch, with steam rising off the crowd. There was no undersoil heating then. This Rangers team was none too subtle and relied on their keeper to hump mile-high balls down the park. With just one bounce on that frozen tundra, the ball was in the Hibs box. No one could control it until one high ball skewed out left. As others backed off, George squinted at the sky and poked out a toe, killing it stone dead. In one movement he slid forward, skipping past Alex MacDonald before Derek Johnstone lunged in from behind to bring George down. Crumpled on top of the ball, George wearily picked himself up and walked over to Johnstone and held out the orange ball. You could imagine his Ulster burr, "Here it is, son. You can have it." A red-faced Johnstone refused the offer. Talk about gratitude.

'George didn't do much else that day but lay on the through ball for the winning goal. It was the pattern for all his games with Hibs, but these few seconds among the dross that made up Premier League matches in 1979/80 were like diamonds in the dust. I saw him against Celtic on 12 January before I returned to London. That day, he scored with a shot that took the Celtic keeper Peter Latchford into the back of the net. Next time I saw him was for the Cup semi-final against Celtic, when I hitched up from London. At Scotch Corner, a white van pulled over. As I jumped in, the driver said, "You're Simon Pia". He'd been at school with my wee brother. Another Hibee, he too was heading for Hampden. The most poignant moment during the 5–0 defeat was when George slipped through a beautiful pass but no Hibs player read it. As he shook his head, Bobby Lennox came over to console George and put an arm around him.

'And that was my last sighting of George in the green until he returned with San Jose Earthquakes. Now, I was a cub reporter and remember the media circus for a Hibs testimonial. The BBC was up from London fighting with us in the tunnel for a few words with yer man and it made the *Nine O'Clock News*. Still, it was an anti-climax. Looking back, these were special days but really, Georgie, we hardly knew ye.'

Tommy Hindley is the man who took the famous picture of George in the Jinglin' Geordie pub back in February 1980. Tommy, who now runs the Professional Sport *picture agency, has never given his version of events on that day until now.*

'It was a commission for a top men's magazine in Norway called *Vi-Menn*, who had arranged for this feature to be done on George Best's time in Scottish football. The journalist came over from Norway and then we both flew up from London to Edinburgh. In the morning, I took some shots of George at the ground: pictures of him training, him with a Hibernian scarf above his head and him standing on the terraces, that kind of stuff. I got on well with him, he was good as gold, a nice, charming bloke.

'After we did the photographs, we went to the pub with the rest of the first-team. We were in the pub from 12.30 p.m. until about 6 p.m., when we had our return flight to London. I suppose the picture was taken pretty late on in the day. George wasn't actually that drunk when I took the photo. Obviously he had had a few drinks by then, but that picture was just one of those frames where the flash caught George with his eyes shut. George had been paid a lot of money to do this interview, but when the time came to do it he had obviously had quite a few drinks and he decided that he didn't want to do it. We parted on good terms; from my point of view it was OK because I had done my photographs, although it was obviously annoying that the journalist didn't get his story.

'At the time I didn't really understand what the implications of that picture really were. Then on the following Sunday night when I was at home, the report came on the TV news saying that George had arrived back at Heathrow Airport after being sacked by Hibernian for failing to turn up for a Scottish Cup match against Ayr United. The story was all about his alcohol problem and how he wanted help from Alcoholics Anonymous. Then I just looked again at that one frame and knew it was a huge news picture. I said to the journalist, "Even though I have taken this shot exclusively for you, in all fairness, this is a news story now and would you mind if I put it out?" So then I went to the *Daily Mirror* and put the print in front of Len Greener, the picture editor back then. He just said, "Don't move from there," and went straight in to show it to the editor. They subsequently ran it exclusively and syndicated it around the world. At the end of the day, as much as I respected George as a player, the fact was that frame was part of George Best's career and had to be used as a news picture.'

Tony Higgins. *Copyright unknown*

Tony Higgins signed for Hibs in 1972 and soon graduated to the first-team, where his bustling, aggressive style and regular goal-scoring exploits made him a favourite with the fans. He joined Partick Thistle in March 1980 and subsequently went on to become boss of the players' union in Scotland. He now works for FIFPro, the World Players Union, and is a regular on the after-dinner speaking circuit.

'No doubt Tom Hart thought that the George Best initiative would bring much-needed glamour to the club, both in terms of attracting more people to the games and also bringing some excitement. At the time, we were languishing at the foot of the table. When the rumours about him coming started, there was a lot of speculation among the players about how much Hibs were paying to bring him to Scotland and there were stories in the press about resentment in the dressing-room, but generally he was well received. There were one or two comments made off the record to the newspapers about his wages and the impact this could have on the team. That created a diversionary story but, no, I don't remember us all sitting down as a squad and saying "Oh what is this guy going to get paid?" Tom Hart promised us that during George's time at the club he would double our bonuses – paid out of the money brought in from the higher attendances. To a degree that took the sting out of the financial discussions and took away any potential resentment. It also helped that George was a decent guy and never played the big star or big personality in the dressing room. So once he got subsumed into the club, he was just treated like everyone else. The dressing-room can be a very hostile environment, with people giving stick to each other. But George just got quietly about his business and had a good laugh with the rest of us.

'Initially he didn't socialise much with us outwith normal hours. George very often didn't even drink alcohol because around that time he was sometimes using these [Antabuse] stomach implants to stop him drinking. But after training he would maybe come with us for a shandy or lemonade when we had a pub lunch in the Jinglin' Geordie. There was maybe seven or eight of us who travelled from Glasgow or Falkirk on the train and we all had a pub lunch with maybe a pint of shandy. After some of the games, George would maybe have a pint or two with us and he would be fine. After the Rangers game, when we beat them 2–1, he came into the Fifty Club across the road and had a few pints with us. It was a good place to go to after the game because no one really bothered or hassled you – and occasionally George would come in there for a quiet pint. I think the problems started when he switched to drinking vodka – that would send him on a different track.

'In the dressing room at that time, I was one of the leading personalities and I suppose I used to pretend that I was like a father figure to him as a kind of joke. I certainly wasn't put in charge of him per se, but people would say to me, "Keep an eye on him when he's out." I didn't feel any great pressure doing that, because when we were out I felt very protective towards him anyway. Occasionally, he would get hassle but not that often, People were more starstruck when they met him. I remember we played Leicester City in a friendly at Easter Road and after the game we went to a nightclub near Waverley Station. That was the first time George had come to a nightclub with us and within five minutes the place was crawling with photographers and there were lots of women wanting to speak to him – it was incredible. At the time he was on the straight and narrow and wasn't drinking, so I said, "George, you'd better get out of here." He took my advice that time – and within ten minutes he was gone.

'His best games for Hibs were when he played a bit deeper. The pace had gone, but he still had good feet. We all remember him for his dribbling wizardry, but what really impressed me about George when I saw him close up was that he could pass a ball so accurately with either foot 30 or 40 yards. Also, his close control was still very good. That day against Rangers at Easter Road was his best performance for Hibs. It was slightly icy, but he still managed to control the ball and pass it so well. The goal I scored that day ended up as being one of the contenders for goal of the season and although it was a good strike by me from 20 yards, it was really all to do with the build up, when George sent a 40-yard pass to Ally Macleod who laid it on to me.'

GEORGE BEST FIRST-TEAM APPEARANCES FOR HIBS

George signing autographs. *Scotsman*

Season 1979–80 – Premier League unless stated otherwise.

Saturday, November 24

St Mirren 2 (Somner 2) Hibernian 1 (Best)

St Mirren – Thomson, Young, Munro, Richardson, Fulton, Copland, Bone, Stark, Somner, McDougall, Abercrombie

Hibernian – McDonald, Brazil, Duncan, Rae, Paterson,

McNamara, Callachan, MacLeod, Ward (Hutchinson), Higgins (McGlinchey), Best

Referee – J. Renton (Cowdenbeath)

Attendance – 13,670

Saturday, December 1

Hibernian 2 (MacLeod, pen, Whittaker, own goal) Partick Thistle 1 (O'Hara)

Hibernian – McArthur, Brazil, Duncan, Rae, Paterson, McNamara, Callachan, MacLeod, Hutchinson, Higgins (Murray), Best

Partick Thistle – Rough, McKinnon (Melrose), Whittaker, Campbell, Anderson, O'Hara, Park, Doyle, Jardine, McAdam, McDonald

Referee – A. McGunnigle (Glasgow)

Attendance – 20,622

Friendly match
Saturday, December 8

Kilmarnock 4 (Houston 2, McDicken, Welsh) Hibernian 0

Kilmarnock – McCulloch, Welsh, Robertson, Clark, Armstrong, McDicken, Houston, Maxwell, Bourke, Mauchlen, Cairney

Hibernian – Nizetic, Brazil, Duncan, Rae, Paterson, McNamara, Callachan (Murray), MacLeod, Hutchinson (Rodier), Campbell (Higgins), Best

Referee – M. Delaney (Airdrie)

Attendance – 4,000

Friendly match
Monday, December 10

Hibernian 3 (MacLeod 3) Leicester City 2 (May, Strickland)

Hibernian – Nizetic, Brazil, Duncan, Rae, Paterson, McNamara, Callachan, Macleod, Hutchinson (Rodier), Campbell, Best

Leicester City – Wallington, Williams, Rofe, Welsh, May, O'Neill, Lineker, Henderson, Young, Byrne, Smith (Sub – Strickland)

Referee – G. B. Smith (Edinburgh)

Attendance: 6,240

Saturday, December 22

Hibernian 2 (Higgins, Campbell) Rangers 1 (McLean)

Hibernian – McArthur, Brazil, Duncan, Rae, Paterson, McNamara, Callachan, McLeod, Higgins, Best

Rangers – Young, Jardine, Dawson, T. Forsyth, Jackson, Stevens, McLean, A. MacDonald (Smith), Johnstone (Cooper), Watson, J. MacDonald

Referee – J. Renton (Cowdenbeath)

Attendance – 18,740

Saturday, January 5

Kilmarnock 3 (Street 3) Hibernian 1 (Campbell)

Kilmarnock – McCulloch, McLean, Welsh, Clark, Armstrong, McDicken, Houston, Gibson, Bourke, Cramond, Street

Hibernian – McArthur, Brazil, Duncan, Rae, Paterson, McNamara, Callachan, Campbell, Higgins, MacLeod, Best

Referee – J. A. R. Wales (Cumbernauld)

Attendance – 6,000

Saturday, January 12

Hibernian 1 (Best) Celtic 1 (Aitken)

Hibernian – McArthur, Brazil, Lambie, Rae, Paterson, McNamara, Callachan, MacLeod, Higgins, Campbell, Best

Celtic – Latchford, Sneddon, McGrain, Aitken, MacDonald, McAdam, Provan, Sullivan, Lennox, MacLeod, Doyle

Referee – B. Robertson (East Kilbride)

Attendance – 21,936

Friendly match
Tuesday, January 15

Leicester City 0 Hibernian 2 (McNamara, Higgins)

Leicester City – Wallington, Williams, Rofe, Goodwin, May, O'Neill, Lineker, Henderson, Young, Kelly, Smith

Hibernian – McArthur, Brazil, Lambie, Rae, Paterson, McNamara, Callachan, MacLeod, Higgins, Campbell, Best

Referee – P. G. Reeves (Leicester)

Scottish Cup – 3rd Round
Saturday, January 26

Meadowbank Thistle 0 Hibernian 1 (Callachan)

Meadowbank Thistle – Neilson, Dunn, Fraser, Boyd, Wight (McGauren), Conroy (Davidson), Small, Leetion, Kelly, Brown, Jobson

Hibernian – McArthur, Brazil, Lambie, Paterson, Stewart, McNamara, Callachan, MacLeod, Higgins, Campbell, Best

Referee – C. J. White (Glasgow)

Attendance – 8,415

Saturday, March 1

Rangers 1 (Johnstone) Hibernian 0

Rangers – McLoy, Jardine, Dawson, Smith, Forsyth, Stevens, Cooper, Russell (A. Macdonald), Johnstone, Redford, J. MacDonald

Hibernian – McArthur, Brazil, Lambie, Cormack, Paterson, Rae, Callachan, MacLeod, Hutchinson, Duncan, Best (Higgins)

Referee – M. Delaney (Cleland)

Attendance – 30,000

Scottish Cup 5ᵗʰ Round
Saturday, March 8

Berwick Rangers 0 Hibernian 0

Berwick Rangers – K. Davidson, Georgeson, McLeod, Moyes, McDowell, Henderson, P. Davidson, Wallace, G. Smith, Romaines, D. Smith

Hibernian – McArthur, Brazil, Lambie, Cormack, Paterson, Rae, Callachan, MacLeod, Higgins, Hutchinson (Murray), Best (Duncan)

Referee – W. Anderson, East Kilbride

Attendance – 7,228

Saturday, March 15

Dundee 3 (Sinclair, Shirra, Ferguson) Hibernian 0

Dundee- Donaldson, McLaren, Schaedler, Millar, Glennie, McGeachie, Mackie, Shirra, Fleming, Sinclair (Ferguson), Corrigan (Murphy)

Hibernian – McArthur, Brazil, Duncan, Paterson, Cormack, Rae, Tierney, MacLeod, Torrance, Campbell, Best

Referee – B. R. McGinlay (Balfron)

Attendance – 8,065

Tuesday, March 25

Hibernian 2 (Best, Murray) Dundee 0

Hibernian – McArthur, Brazil, Duncan, Tierney, Rae, McNamara, Murray, Cormack, Torrance (Hutchinson), Campbell, Best

Dundee – Donaldson, Barr, Schaedler, McLaren, McGeachie, Shirra, Mackie, Millar, Fleming, Sinclair, Corrigan (Murphy)

Referee – T. Kellock, East Kilbride

Attendance – 5,000

Saturday, March 29

Celtic 4 (Lennox, pen, McGarvey, Doyle, McDonald) Hibernian 0

Celtic – Latchford, McGrain, MacLeod, Aitken, McDonald, McAdam, Provan, Casey (Burns), McGarvey, Lennox, Doyle

Hibernian – McArthur, Brazil, Duncan, Tierney (Callachan), Rae, McNamara (Hutchinson), Murray, Cormack, Torrance, Campbell, Best

Referee – T. Muirhead (Stenhousemuir)

Attendance – 22,000

Wednesday, April 2

Hibernian 0 Dundee United 2 (Dodds, Pettigrew)

Hibernian – McArthur, Brazil, Duncan, Rae, Paterson, Tierney (Callachan), Murray, Campbell, Torrance, Cormack, Best

Dundee United – McAlpine, Stark, Kopel, Phillip, Hegarty, Narey, Dodds, Sturrock, Pettigrew (Payne), Holt, Kirkwood

Referee – H. Alexander (Irvine)

Attendance – 5,000

Saturday, April 5

St Mirren 2 (Logan, Richardson) Hibernian 0

St Mirren – Thomson, Beckett, Munro, Richardson, Fulton, Copland, Bone, Stark, Somner, Weir, Logan

Hibernian – McArthur, Brazil, Rae, Paterson (Duncan), Stewart, Cormack, Campbell, MacLeod, Torrance, Tierney, Best

Referee – A. C. Harris (Dundee)

Attendance – 4,000

Scottish Cup Semi-Final
Saturday, April 12 at Hampden Park

Celtic 5 (Lennox, Provan, Doyle, MacLeod, McAdam,)
Hibernian 0

Celtic – Latchford, Sneddon, McGrain, Aitken, McDonald, McAdam, Provan, Lennox (Burns), McGarvey, MacLeod, Doyle (McLuskey)

Hibernian – McArthur, Brazil, Duncan, McNamara, Stewart, Rae, Callachan, Torrance, Campbell, Paterson, Best

Referee – B. R. McGinlay (Balfron)

Attendance – 32,925

Wednesday, April 16

Aberdeen 1 (Watson) Hibernian 1 (Rae)

Aberdeen – Clark, Kennedy, McMaster, McLeish, Rougvie, Miller, Strachan, Archibald, McGhee (Hamilton), Jarvie, Scanlon (Watson)

Hibernian – McArthur, McNamara, Duncan, Paterson, Stewart, Rae, Callachan, Lambie, Torrance (MacLeod), Hutchinson, Best

Referee – D. Murdoch (Bothwell)

Attendance – 16,000

Saturday, April 19

Hibernian 0 Dundee United 2 (Pettigrew, Bannon)

Hibernian – McArthur, McNamara, Lambie, Paterson, Stewart, Rae (Cormack), Callachan, Murray, MacLeod, Hutchinson (Torrance), Best

Dundee United – McAlpine, Stark, Kopel, Phillip, Hegarty, Narey, Bannon, Sturrock, Pettigrew, Holt, Dodds

Referee – H. Alexander (Irvine)

Attendance – 4,921

Tuesday, September 9

Dundee 1 (Scrimgeour) Hibernian 2 (MacLeod, G. Rae)

Dundee – Geddes, Barr, Schaedler, Scrimgeour, Glennie, McGeachie, Mackie, Scott, Sinclair, Ferguson, Shirra

Hibernian – McArthur, Brown, Duncan, McNamara, Stewart, Callachan, Hamil (Jamieson), G. Rae, MacLeod, Connolly, Best

Referee – J. Duncan (Gorebridge)

Saturday, September 20

Hamilton Accies 1 (Graham) Hibernian 1 (Connolly)

Hamilton Accies – Ferguson, Frew, Brown, Alexander, McDougall, Marshall, McDowall, McManus, Fairlie, McAdams, McGrogan (Subs, Wright, Howie)

Hibs – McArthur, Brown, Duncan, McNamara, Paterson, Callachan, Hamill, Rae, MacLeod, Connolly, Best (Subs, Torrance, Cormack)

Referee – J. A. R. Wales (Cumbernauld)

Bell's League Cup 3rd Round – 1st leg
Wednesday, September 24

Hibernian 2 (Jamieson 2) Clyde 1 (Ahern, pen)
(Aggregate score – Hibernian 4 Clyde 1)

Hibernian – McArthur, Brown, Duncan, McNamara, Paterson, Callachan, Jamieson, Rae, MacLeod, Connolly, Best

Clyde – McWilliams, Brogan (Edgar), Filippi, Dempsey, Boyd, Ahern, Kean, O'Neill, Masterton, Hyslop (Dolan), McAlpine

Referee – I. M. Foote (Glasgow)

Saturday, October 4

Dunfermline 0 Hibernian 2 (MacLeod 2)

Dunfermline – Whyte, Thomson, Mercer, Salton, A. Robertson, Hegarty, McNaughton, B. Robertson, Leonard, Donnelly, O'Brien

Hibernian – McArthur, Brown, Duncan, McNamara, Paterson, Callachan, Jamieson (Wilson), Rae, MacLeod, Connolly, Best

Referee – B. R. McGinley (Balfron)

Attendance – 8,000

Bell's League Cup quarter-final – 1st leg
Wednesday, October 8

Ayr United 2 (Frye 2) Hibernian 2 (Wilson, Macleod)

Ayr United – Rennie, Shanks, Nicol, McSherry, Hendry, Fleeting, Frye, Love, Morris, Connor, Christie

Hibernian – McArthur, Brown, Duncan, McNamara, Paterson, Callachan, Jamieson, Rae, McLeod, Connolly, Best

Referee – R. B. Valentine (Dundee)

Attendance – 4, 717

Saturday, October 11

Hibernian 2 Falkirk 0 (Connolly, Jamieson)

Hibernian – McArthur, Brown, Duncan, McNamara, Paterson, Callachan, Wilson (Jamieson), Rae, MacLeod, Connolly, Best

Falkirk – Allan, Hoggan, Nicol (Spence), Brown, Oliver, McRoberts, Leetion (Watson), Herd, Thomson, Stevenson, Conn

Referee – W. Knowles (Inverurie)

Attendance – 6,947

Bibliography

Books

Rothman's Football Yearbook 1980–81, editor: Jack Rollin, Queen Anne Press, 1980

The Hibees, John R. Mackay, John Donald Publishing, 1986

Sunshine on Leith, Simon Pia, Mainstream, 1995

Bestie: A Portrait of a Legend, George Best and Joe Lovejoy, Sidgwick and Jackson, 1998

Blessed: The Autobiography, George Best and Ray Collins, Ebury Press, 2001

George and Me: My Autobiography, Angie Best with Nicola Pittam, Virgin Books, 2001

The Men Who Made Hibernian FC since 1946, Jim Jeffrey, Tempus Publishing, 2005

Hard Tackles and Dirty Baths: The Inside Story of Football's Golden Era, George Best and Harry Harris, Ebury Press, 2005

Having a Ball, Eddie Turnbull and Martin Hannan, Mainstream, 2006

Our George: A Family Memoir, Barbara Best with Lindy McDowell, Gill & McMillan, 2007

The Don: The Willie Miller Story, Willie Miller and Rob Robertson, Birlinn, 2007

Flawed Genius: Scottish Football's Self-Destructive Mavericks, Stephen McGowan, Birlinn, 2009 – contains a chapter on George's time in Edinburgh.

Newspaper Articles

Edinburgh Evening News, 18 September 1970: 'The man who will put Hart into Hibs' by Hamish Coghill

Edinburgh Evening News, 7 November 1979: 'Fulham OK Hibs bid to approach Best' by Stewart Brown

The Scotsman, 12 November 1979: 'Best likes the Hibs set-up' by Ian Wood

Edinburgh Evening News, 14 November 1979: 'Best says "I want to play for Hibs"' by Stewart Brown

The Scotsman, 17 November 1979: 'Signing of Best is an inspired venture' by Ian Wood

Edinburgh Evening News, 21 November 1979: 'The girl who is more than a match for George' by Jane Ellison

The Scotsman, 3 December 1979: 'George Best spreads the good cheer' by Ian Wood

The Scotsman, 14 January 1980: 'Best is a genius – Turnbull'

The Scotsman, 11 February 1980: 'Best back in Edinburgh'

The Glasgow Herald, 18 February 1980 'Hibs sack George Best' by Alan MacDermid, Tom McConnell and Hamish Leal

Edinburgh Evening News, 18 February 1980: 'Best's drinking spree costs him £40,000' by Stewart Brown

Edinburgh Evening News, 23 February 1980: 'Best can come back, says Hart' by Stewart Brown

Edinburgh Evening News, 28 February 1980: 'Best: I feel that I'm winning the battle'

Observer Sports Monthly, 2 March 2003: 'My team: Hibernian' by Dougray Scott

The Sunday Times, 9 March 2003: 'Caught in time: George Best joins Hibs' by Mike Wilson

The Scotsman, 3 December 2005: 'A bigger legend than the Stone of Scone' by Alan Pattullo

Stornoway Gazette, 16 June 2008: 'Field of Memories – Colin Campbell'

The Herald, 3 October 2008: 'Jock Wilson obituary' by David Torrance

INDEX

Note: **Matches played** are listed by competition under **Hibernian's matches.**